G000165644

TO BLACK PARENTS
VISITING EARTH

Also by Janet Stickmon:

Crushing Soft Rubies—A Memoir

Midnight Peaches, Two O'Clock Patience—
A Collection of Essays, Poems, and Short Stories
on Womanhood and the Spirit

TO BLACK PARENTS VISITING EARTH

Raising Black Children in the 21st Century

JANET STICKMON

BROKEN SHACKLE PUBLISHING • El Cerrito

Copyright © 2018 Janet Stickmon

BROKEN SHACKLE PUBLISHING
International
P.O. Box 861
El Cerrito, CA 94530
www.brokenshackle.net

All rights reserved. No part of this book may be reproduced, reprinted, or used in any form, including via electronic or mechanical means, now known or created hereafter; this includes no photocopying, scanning, recording, or use of any information storage or retrieval system, without the written consent of the author.

Publisher's Cataloging-in-Publication Data

Names: Stickmon, Janet, author.
Title: To Black parents visiting Earth : raising Black children in the 21st century / Janet Stickmon.
Description: Includes bibliographical references. | El Cerrito, CA: Broken Shackle Publishing, International, 2019.
Identifiers: LCCN 2017919090 | ISBN 978-0-9759908-5-8 (pbk.) | 978-0-9759908-6-5 (epub)
Subjects: LCSH Stickmon, Janet. | African American parents--Biography. | African American children. | Child rearing--United States. | African American parents. | Parent and child--United States. | African American children--Ethnic identity. | African American children--Psychology. | United States--Race relations. | African Americans--Race identity. | African American children--Education. | BISAC BIOGRAPHY & AUTOBIOGRAPHY / Personal Memoirs | BIOGRAPHY & AUTOBIOGRAPHY / Cultural, Ethnic & Regional / African American & Black | FAMILY & RELATIONSHIPS / Parenting / General. | SOCIAL SCIENCE / Ethnic Studies / African American Studies.
Classification: LCC E185.86 .S763 2019 | DDC 306.85/08996073--dc23

Notice
The information given here is designed to offer a perspective that will add to the discourse related to parenting, race, self-care, and education. It is not intended as a substitute for any professional legal, medical, or psychiatric treatment. If you suspect you have a legal, medical, or mental health problem or concern, please seek competent, professional assistance. Mention of specific companies, organizations, artists, or authorities in this book does not imply that they endorse this book, its author, or the publisher.

Library of Congress Control Number: 2017919090
ISBN 978-0-9759908-5-8

The broken shackle logo is a trademark of Broken Shackle Publishing, International owned by Janet Stickmon.
Front Cover Photograph: © 2017 Janet Stickmon
Back Cover Image: © 2016 Roy Miles Jr.
Cover Design: © 2018 Design Action Collective

to my husband Shawn Taylor

ACKNOWLEDGMENTS

Thank you to God and all the ancestors whose guidance and love allow me to enjoy countless blessings in life. Thank you to: my parents Lucrecia and Fermon Stickmon; the parents of my adult life, Vangie Buell and Tom Shepardson; to both Vangie and Bill Buell for being such loving grandparents to my daughter; the Stickmon Family, the Adderly Family, the Rodriguez Family, and the Shepardson Family; Willie Cobb, Edwin Lozada, Jennifer Carlin, Edward Beanes, Roberto-Juan Gonzalez, Enid Gonzalez, Jennifer King, Michelle Lee, Georgina Perez, Orlando Carreon, Alex Guerrero, Carlos Hagedorn, Curtis Acosta, Mel Orpilla, Dawn Mabalon, Kevin Nadal, Meg Lemke, Wade Nobles, Sheikh Ibrahim Abdurrahman Farajajé, Yeye Luisah Teish, Sr. Eva Lumas, Fr. Jesse Montes, and Fr. Patrick Mullen. To the Filipino American National Historical Society (FANHS) for supporting my work from the very beginning. Thank you to Roy Miles Jr. for your artwork in the book cover, stickers, buttons, and T-shirts. Thank you to Poonam Whabi for your book cover design. To Gloria Ladson-Billings, Kiese Laymon, and Andrew Jolivette, thank you for taking the time to read my book and write such beautiful blurbs. Your insights and honesty have inspired and strengthened me and countless others over the years; I am honored and humbled by your words. Thank you to my husband, Shawn Taylor, and our beautiful daughter who inspire me, make me laugh, keep me strong, and always remind me of what's important in life.

Thank you to all the donors including: Ashay by the Bay, Christina Andrada, Jennifer Carlin, Orlando Carreon, Catherine Choy, Tyler Cohen, Oscar De Haro, Andrew Demons, Heidi Durrow, Nicole Gardner, Jennifer Gholap, Shannon Gibney, D'vorah Grenn, Rudy Guevarra, Carlos Hagedorn, Lori Hanson, Abraham Ignacio, Mel Lagasca, Elizabeth Lawrence, Meg Lemke, Ron Lopez, Dawn Mabalon, Oonagh Mahnke, Lisa Suguitan Melnick, Michael Noll, Ariana Perry, Liberty Rapada, Tony Robles, Jennifer Selby, Beth Simpson, and Keno Tesoro

Special thanks to *Silver Time Bender* donors: Craig Alimo, Michelle Bautista, Robin Cooper, Elinor Crescenzi, Herna Cruz-Louie, E.J.R. David, François Pincemin, and Tom Shepardson

CONTENTS

LETTER #1

February 28, 2015

To Black Parents Visiting Earth,

It has taken me several months to write to you…and I don't even know your name…or if you'll be visiting my part of the planet. I guess it's taken forever because this stuff is too close to my heart and therefore very difficult to empty onto paper. But I wanted to write you anyway just to make sure you and the family would be okay. I know we've never met, but I think about your safety. I think about your children's safety.

I'm over here in North America, not too far from 38° N, 122° W. Though much of what I'll share will be helpful to you no matter where you are in the world, there will be some details that may be specific to this area…and it's for this reason I hope that other Black parents around the world will also write to you.

This will be the first of several letters I'll send your way. Hopefully, you'll receive them all. You can think of them as a love letter-life guide to Black parents. Truly, those parents who aren't Black but have Black children can benefit from these letters as well.

But right now, my heart is with other Black parents: those who look at their child's skin—from dark black to olive—and see their own. It's for those parents who feel Africa shining through their child's waves and naps and see that this is the same Africa that shines through their own hair.

These letters are for those of us who have old wounds that get reopened every time our children's capabilities are underestimated, every time our children get excluded from a game, every time our children are teased about their hair, every time our children are hit, kicked, or pushed by a white child, or every time our children get harassed, beaten, or killed by the police. These are some of the things your children will encounter when you come to Earth—the things that over time can cause our babies to question their very humanity.

Family, I write these letters to you. What I will share with you may save your life and your sanity—not to mention your child's. And if it doesn't, well then, at least it will save you time.

This love letter-life guide begins with more questions than answers. I ask myself daily how I should raise my 6-year-old daughter to love being Black as well as being Filipino, Puerto Rican, and Jamaican? Are my husband and I doing a good enough job helping her understand the impact of white supremacy on the world, while keeping her from getting consumed by it to the point of debilitation? Will my child know that she is capable of being a scientist if she is only complimented for the way her body moves? How do I convince my child that her hair is beautiful when people call her hair wild, wiry, and bushy everyday?

My husband and I have found some answers to these questions; we had to because Baby Girl's survival and sanity depended on it. Baby Girl must learn (or at least be familiar with) the ways of white, male, upper/middle class, Christian, straight, cisgender, able-bodied folk because she is surrounded by these spheres of influence and will be judged daily by how well she adheres to their spoken and unspoken standards that even they are sometimes unaware of.

I want Baby Girl—my firecracker, my spark plug—to continue being the compassionate, talkative, goofy, quick-witted, feisty, funny, smart child that she's always been. Though we're not experts, I think my husband and I are doing a great job making this happen, especially considering all we've exposed her to, all the conversations we've had, and all the laughs we've shared.

But, I must admit that I'm tired. Molding counterhegemonic armor for a 6-year-old child, making sure it is small and light enough for her to wear, is some kind of sick, warped task Black parents perform daily without exploding. Meanwhile, the white world remains clueless about how our time is spent. There are many hours in my day when I resent the burden of this task. But I will continue to do it for my daughter's protection, especially if it means my work will preserve her silly laugh and bright eyes.

I am determined to spare my daughter the hatred I harbored toward my own Blackness when I was growing up. That self-loathing—the anguish, the disappointment, the disgust—was beyond unnecessary. I want to ensure that Baby Girl develops a love for her nut brown glow, her African halo of hair, and all the rest of her that is African and African American in heart and spirit. In order to cultivate this self-love, as her parents, we need to make sure she is surrounded by positive reflections of herself in classrooms, libraries, universities, and businesses; in books, television, billboards, and magazines; in toys (and packaging for toys), children's websites, and apps. She needs to know she comes from a long line of authors, scientists, healers, political leaders, artists, and more. She needs to know that she, I, we exist.

After the death of my parents during my teenage years, I went many nights feeling alone, vulnerable, and unsupported, cradled only by nightmares of being forever abandoned and forgotten. Though I had relatives who did their best to provide me with food and shelter, laughter and love—gifts I will always be grateful for—there was something else my heart needed that I couldn't give words to.

Years later, I realized what I needed was protection, or better yet, security. I needed a security rooted in the part of my bloodline that the world would see as all too powerful—so powerful, the world would inflict the most toxic, unwarranted pain upon it to erase all evidence of its existence, and then be free to walk in daylight with impunity and step into the spotlight for applause.

This security needed to be born from within the heart—the heart being known to the Yoruba as *"okan,"* the seat of emotions, thought, and action.[1] I envision this security being a force field emerging from my *okan,* spreading all around it to protect it from harm but still allowing love to enter.

I had no instruction manual to use when I was both mother and father to myself. I suppose subconsciously I created a force field for my *okan* as I daydreamt about what my future would look like: what university I'd attend, what profession I'd undertake. I dreamt of ways I would protect and defend my own child if I were a parent. I imagined the ways I would help her maintain pride in her African American heritage and all other parts of her heritage.

Now, here I am: a mother. I love my daughter. I will do everything I can to protect her. But I also know I must teach her how to defend herself and how to find love and security within. I learn how to do this everyday; and often Baby Girl is my teacher.

So, in my next few letters, I will share with you what I've learned about instilling love and security in my own child. May your children find the resilience, confidence, and pride to silence the nightmares I pray they never have.

With love,

Janet Stickmon

---

[1] Babasehinde A. Ademuleya, "The Concept of Ori in the Traditional Yoruba Visual Representation of Human Figures," *Nordic Journal of African Studies,* 2007, http://www.njas.helsinki.fi/pdf-files/vol16num2/ademuleya.pdf.

LETTER #2: BOOKS

March 9, 2015

Dear Black Parents Visiting Earth:

Long before those early months of motherhood, when I was trying to figure out how to nurse Baby Girl, how to change her diaper, how to swaddle her, and how to get the child to nap in her crib, I knew she needed to be inoculated against the self-hatred that might potentially plague her.

So, before my husband and I even chose her name, the inoculation started when we decided to buy her African and African American children's books. I was 11 weeks pregnant when I began our collection with a handful of books from Ashay by the Bay owned by vendor Deborah Day at the Ashby Flea Market in Berkeley. By the time Baby Girl was born, our collection included books like *Shades of Black—A Celebration of Our Children*, *I Like Myself*, *Please, Baby, Please*, and *Book of Black Heroes: Scientists, Healers and Inventors*. These were among several books we read to her while she was still in the womb.

Within just a few years, our African and African American book collection grew to include *Abiyoyo*, *Anansi the Spider—A Tale from the Ashanti*, *Ashanti to Zulu—African Traditions*, *Barack Obama: Son of Promise*, *Brown Sugar Fairies*, *Child of Hope*, *Corduroy*, *Cornrows*, *Fish for the Grand Lady*, *Furqan's First Flat Top*, *George Washington Carver* (by Tonya Bolden), *God's Dream*, *Grandpa's Visit*, *Hair Dance*, *I am Mixed*, *Jazzy Miz Mozetta*, *The Jewel Fish of Karnak*, *Letter to Benjamin Banneker*, *Mandela: From the Life of the South African Statesman*, *Mansa Musa*, *The Moon Ring*, *Mufaro's Beautiful Daughters*, *My Very Breast Friend*, *Pathfinders: The Journeys of 16 Extraordinary Black Souls*, *Schomburg: The Man Who Built a Library*,

The Sound of Kwanzaa, Thunder Rose, Wangari's Trees of Peace: A True Story from Africa, Welcome to Zanzibar Road, When the Beat was Born—DJ Kool Herc and the Creation of Hip Hop, and *Young Pele: Soccer's First Star*. Our collection also includes children's stories from other ethnic groups from both within and outside of Baby Girl's multiracial mosaic. We've found that this gives her a broader understanding of the similarities and differences between their/our experiences, helps her develop a certain level of solidarity and kinship with people of various ethnic backgrounds, and allows her to understand and be proud of her identity as a multiracial child.

I recommend you begin your collection as soon as you arrive. You'll have a hard time finding many of these books in major bookstores like Barnes and Nobles or even some of the independent bookstores like Pegasus Books and Half Price Books. If you land near 38° N, 122° W, Ashay by the Bay in Berkeley and Marcus Books Stores in Oakland are great places to start. If you land near 34° N, 118° W, visit Eso Won Books in Los Angeles. Online, you can visit Marcusbookstores.com and Esowonbookstore.com. When in doubt, you can always try Amazon.com too.

If your child is learning to read and do basic math, I recommend Starfall.com. I was surprised to find that unlike other reading/math websites and LeapPad learning game cartridges, the majority of the images of children used in Starfall were Black and Brown children. So, so rare! What a treasure!

Yes, I am excited, and yet I am saddened by the thought that I am elated to find crumbs to satisfy my hunger. Though images of Black and Brown children on reading/math websites, apps, etc. are rare, truly, they shouldn't be…not in the 21st century.

In any case, as your child advances and begins reading chapter books, look for *Dactyl Hill Squad, The Great Cake Mystery: Precious Ramotswe's Very First Case, Keena Ford and the Field Trip Mix-up, Jupiter Storm, Keena Ford and the Secret Journal Mix-Up, Kid Caramel—Case of the Missing Ankh, Lulu and the Dog from the Sea, The Magical Adventures of Pretty Pearl, Midnight and the Man Who Had No Tears, Midnight and Little Girl Blue*, and *Sage Carrington—Eighth Grade Science Sleuth*.

Also check out comic books and graphic novels like *Brother Man: Dictator of Discipline*, *Niobe: She is Life*, *Goldie Vance*, *Lumberjanes*, *Cloudia and Rex*, *Akissi*, and *Maximum Ride*.

Before our daughter was old enough to read on her own, we read most of these books to her before bedtime. Other times, we took turns reading paragraphs during the day so she could have the chance to practice reading beyond her grade level. She enjoyed being read to but didn't always enjoy reading; early on, she found it quite frustrating. But I am happy to say that by the end of the second grade, she was able to read at the fourth grade level.

Thanks to all those years of reading to her at bedtime, visiting bookstores, having her read 15-20 minutes a day (or 2-3 times a day in the summer), attending school book fairs (where her classmates' excitement over books was downright contagious), going to comic book festivals like the Black Comix Arts Festival in San Francisco (which her Daddy cofounded), Baby Girl developed a genuine love for reading. She is now reading all kinds of chapter books, comic books, and graphic novels without much chiding from Mama and Daddy. I hope that your child will enjoy reading just as much as ours does.

*

Final note. In kindergarten, Baby Girl brought home *Christmas in Camelot* and was talking a lot about some child named *Junie B. Jones*. When I saw the covers of these books, I thought, *Damn, it's a good thing we have all these Black books at home! I wonder how many more books it'll take to outweigh the flood of white people books she'll read at school.* Then, I began to question why my child must wait until she comes home before she hears and reads stories that reflect herself and her ancestors.

Our books need to be in school libraries, on classroom bookshelves, in mainstream bookstores, and integrated into the school curriculum for all students to benefit from. Many of us on Earth have been trying to make this a reality for at least a couple centuries. There have been modest successes and much struggle. Dare systems on Earth wait for the intergalactic unification of Black people before it is forced to make the structural change that white supremacy dreads?! Perhaps, that's what it will take. I don't know. If so, then I hope we can rely on your help upon your arrival.

For now, just be safe and take care.

Your Sister in Spirit,

Janet

LETTER #3: HAIR

March 31, 2015

To Black Parents Visiting Earth:

It took many jars of relaxing cream and scabs on my scalp before I stopped strangling Africa. The day I stopped putting chemicals in my hair was the day I began loving it for being natural.

Despite my Filipino mother's attempt to get me to love my hair (as she gently ran my fingers through my scalp to feel the beauty of my own waves and curls), I was still subject to the world's disgust with Black hair—a world today that has plenty of Korean-owned Black hair shops where you're sure to find Cream of Nature and aisles of Indian Remy hair but never find Sheba Locks and Miss Jessie's; a world where Gabby Douglas is condemned by Black folk for the appearance of her hair as opposed to being praised for her feats as an Olympian.

In 2011, I wrote an essay called "Locks" that describes the journey that led me to decide to lock my hair in 2005. Below is an excerpt that explains what messages Black women receive about our natural hair:

> There are systems in place that communicate to the world that long, straight, flowing hair that blows in the wind is the standard against which all other hair types ought to be measured and evaluated. Though it may be true that those with straight and/or limp hair receive the message that having more body or wave to one's hair is more desirable, one must take a close look at how prevalent such messages are in comparison to the implicit and explicit messages (from within and outside our race) that bombard Black women and girls, telling us that straight hair is not only preferable

and normative, but anything other than straight is deviant, dirty, messy, and akin to pubic hair. These judgments don't stop at your physical appearance, but they also imply that your inner way of being is just as dirty and deviant. Secondly, there is a big difference between telling women that hair with more body and wave is beautiful and telling women that coarse, kinky, or nappy hair is beautiful. Ads, for example, that implicitly or explicitly promote hair with more body and wave (or maybe even ringlets, too) communicate the message that it's okay to have some waves, but if it's too curly and too frizzy at the same time, you are on the brink of creeping into ugly territory! Such messages are communicated through casual conversation, jokes, silent stares of contempt, magazines, music videos, television, Korean-owned and Black-owned hair supply stores, billboards, cinema, dolls, greeting cards, the Internet, and much more. Never had I researched how to straighten and damage my hair through the use of a chemical relaxer, hairdryer, hot comb, or curling iron. Nonetheless, this came quite naturally to me considering what was readily available; I was provided with plenty of assistance. Over the years, however, becoming aware of how I internalized these destructive external messages put me in a better position to actively choose to reject such messages and begin to understand my hair. How strange it is to realize that in my thirties I must *learn* from books how to take care of my natural hair.[2]

I wrote this when Baby Girl was about 3-4 years old. I had a clear sense of what my daughter would encounter. Around this time whenever my daughter's hair was in braids or twists, people didn't say too much about her hair—good or bad. But when she wore it down, people had all kinds of things to say, and here's just a taste:

➤ White adults (who believed they were complimenting her): "Wow, your hair's so cool. It's so wild!" or "I wish I could be that free," or "It looks like a cloud."

➤ Older Black women (usually with disdain): "Why don't you do something with that hair?" or "You need to moisturize that hair."

➤ White adults (often enthusiastic women): "Nice hair" or "I like your hair."

---

[2] Janet Stickmon, *Midnight Peaches, Two O'clock Patience* (Oakland: Broken Shackle Publishing, International, 2011), 78-79.

> ➤ Young Black women (usually with their own hair worn natural): "Go 'head lil' mama! Your hair is so beautiful!" or "Let your crown go!"

Hearing these things, particularly the countless negative, ignorant comments outweighing the number of affirmations, came as no surprise.

Baby Girl was small with a sweet mind filled with popsicles, playgrounds, and confetti; I could barely imagine how she was making sense of the world's preoccupation with her hair. I would need to explain this to her; my husband would need to explain this to her. But for the time being, we reveled in moments when young sistahs told her how beautiful her hair was. Baby Girl could count on this love at places and events like Juneteenth celebrations or the Ashby Flea Market in Berkeley or the Malcolm X Jazz Festival or the Life is Living Festival in Oakland. Such environments were sparse but served as just enough medicine for the sickness that suggested her hair was abnormal and in need of being tamed.

She continued hearing a strange mix of insults and awkward comments about her hair throughout her preschool years. But when she started kindergarten, it was a whole different game.

*

For the first few months of kindergarten, I styled my daughter's hair in braids and twists because I was afraid of subjecting her to more ignorance at this majority white private school.

On November 22, 2013, my daughter wore her hair down for the first time at school. As soon as she walked through the gate to sign in, a white female student (from the middle school classroom) came up from behind and said, "Oh your hair is so springy!" and began to touch my daughter's hair. I fought the urge to slap the girl's hand and decided to see how my daughter would handle this.

Baby Girl never turned around. She ignored the girl as she signed in. I don't know why, and I didn't ask. I just hugged and kissed her and left for work, knowing that we needed to discuss this after school.

When I held her before leaving that morning, I didn't want her to feel my tears and rage. I wanted her to know that I loved her deeply. I wanted her to know that I understood that her beauty was too fluid, too big for some to fully comprehend…that she will encounter many with little to no experience with Black people and because of this, they will not know how to properly admire and respect her beauty. That morning, I don't remember if I held her tighter than usual, but I hope I did. And I don't know if my kisses felt richer and more meaningful, but I hope they did. All I'm sure about is that my daughter knows me well; there were many times in her early life when she consoled me. There were many times when I tried to hide my face only for her to see through, within, and beyond me. Though I asked no questions and gave no lecture, I left wondering what she knew about my silence. And I wondered what wisdom she carried in her backpack that day.

*

I picked her up from school.
We sat in my car.
I pieced together my thoughts.

    "So, um…how did it feel when that girl touched your hair this morning?"
    "I don't know."
    "She didn't even ask if she could touch your hair," I said, knowing damn well that asking wouldn't have made it okay, but the more I thought about it, the fact that she didn't ask just made it even worse.
    "But Mama, she did ask permission."
    "Baby Girl, no, she didn't. I was right there."

Alright. Now, I was already upset about the hair-touching and the not-asking, but now it seemed like my daughter was lying for this girl. Sure, psychologists and pediatricians and sociologists and teachers could come up with a rationale for what was happening. Hell, I could come up with some quick explanations if it was happening to somebody else's kid. But in that moment, the first thought that came to mind was *What the fuck?!* Either she wanted to protect this girl or she just didn't want me to be angry or was afraid that the white teen might come after her. Or maybe a little bit of all of this. I wasn't completely sure. Whatever the case, ultimately it appeared as though she was trying to protect the white student. I knew far too many cases of Black folk covering for or making excuses for the conscious and unconscious wrongs of white folk and even though Baby Girl was just a child, it was important for her to understand that she should not make up anything to cover up anyone's wrongdoing.

"Did anyone else at school say something about your hair?"

"Yes. Bethany called my hair bushy."

You know, I have never had a reputation for being a hothead—not a habitual hothead anyway. But when someone says or does something that hurts your child, there is something primal within a mama's heart that makes her want to snatch somebody's kneecaps off.

The first time I felt the true strength of this protective impulse was when Baby Girl was barely two months old. We were at the park, and I was pushing her in the stroller. A squirrel came out of the bushes a little too fast, stopped, and crept a little too close to the stroller. I watched it carefully and thought, *If that thing jumps on my baby, I swear I'll turn the damn squirrel into a sweater!*

Anyways, that's how I felt. The hair-touching. The not-asking. The cover-up. Baby's hair was springy, and now it's bushy too?!

The words of Frantz Fanon, Homi K. Bhabha, and Edward Said were jumbled up in my head like those wordballs in *Electric Company*. Their work on "otherness" lived in my mind, but as I sat in the car, I struggled to translate their words into a language that this 5-year-old could embrace. Luckily before she was born, my husband and I laid down a foundation that would allow her to understand.

One of Baby Girl's middle names is Assegai.[3] When we gave her this name, we wanted to make sure she was in a position to engage in emotional and physical combat. Whether it be the traditional *assegai*—a long-shafted, throwing spear used by the Zulu (prior to Shaka Zulu's reign) and other Nguni clans—or the broad-bladed, short stabbing *assegai*, known as the *iKlwa*—Shaka Zulu's innovation, making the *assegai* effective in close combat—I wanted her to be equipped with the will to fight to defend and preserve her self-dignity and the dignity of others who suffer injustice.[4]

I looked at her eyes. Her hair. Her face. I asked God why she must wield her spear so early in life. I gently placed the *assegai* in her hand and wept inside.

"Baby Girl, your hair is beautiful. It is African. It is natural, beautiful, and free. If someone tries to touch your hair, say, "Please don't touch my hair, you don't know me well enough to touch my hair.""

She quickly held the *assegai*, "Ok, Mama. And Mama, then I'll just go like this," and she did a little bob and weave move as if avoiding a blow to the head.

I giggled, "Yes, you can do that too."

There were many other incidents related to my daughter's hair at that school. The need for education about Black hair was apparent. The other incidents took place a year later when Baby Girl entered the first grade. Students continued to make fun of her hair. There were also children who insisted they had the right to touch her hair even when she told them not to.

---

[3] Anthropologist Eileen Krige uses the *assegai* as a generic term for spear and lists several types of *assegais* used by the Zulu. The long-shafted, throwing spear is specifically named the *inCusa*. See Eileen Krige, *Social System of the Zulus* (New York: Longmans, Green, & Co., 1936), 400-401.

[4] Brian Roberts, *The Zulu Kings* (London: Sphere Books Limited, 1977), 48; Donald R. Morris, *The Washing of the Spears: The Rise and Fall of the Zulu Nation* (London: Pimlico, 1994), 37-47; Eileen J. Krige, *Social System of the Zulus* (New York: Longmans, Green, & Co., 1936), 400-401.

There were Baby Girl's tears. There were talks with teachers and parents. There were sincere apologies. Heavy apologies. Empty and awkward apologies. Sympathetic emails. Stupid emails. "Good" intentions obscured by big egos. In the name of inclusivity, white people using API folks as a bludgeon to silence Black folks. Racism exposed, quickly followed by textbook cases of white women's tears. People of color showing solidarity. White allies quick to listen and quick to act. Baby Girl defending her dignity with punches and kicks. Mama and Daddy hugging Baby, telling her how beautiful her skin and hair are…all of this in between reading time and math worksheets.

Though I was pleased with the support from the head of school, her teachers, and the afterschool care providers, the ignorant reactions to my daughter's hair kept coming, and I was tired. I couldn't just stand by and let my daughter wait until the next student said something stupid about her hair.

Since I was already planning to come in to do a Kwanzaa presentation, I asked my daughter's lower elementary teacher (equivalent to grades 1-3 in public school) if I could come in to do a presentation about Black hair. She loved the idea and welcomed me to the class. Later, I was also invited to do the same presentation for the kindergarten class.

I began with reading *Hair Dance* (the book that inspired me to see Baby Girl's hair as a halo). I spoke about the many textures of Black hair, ranging from straight and wavy to coarse and tight curls. I pointed to a display of illustrations and photos of Black women as I described various Black hairstyles like afros, afro puffs, cornrows, locks, twists, and African thread wrapping. I explained that it's important not to refer to Black hair as wild, springy, frizzy, bushy, or wiry.[5] Our hair is curly, beautiful, and African. If someone with straight hair wants to compliment our hair, they can simply say, "I like your hair," and leave it at that. "Don't try to touch it," I said. Or

---

[5] No one asked why, but if they did, I was ready to explain—using age-appropriate language—that such words carry a negative connotation and suggest an inferiority to straight hair; in short, not only are these words unflattering, but are also insulting.

else your hand might get slapped. Well, I didn't say that part. I was thinking it, though.

I ended the presentation with a little skit using two stuffies: a Black doll named Imani and a white poodle named Molly. Imani approaches Molly, talking about how cute she is and reaches out to pet her. I asked the children to imagine how some of us might do this when we see a cute dog. Then I said, "What if one of us saw Imani's hair and tried to touch it because we admired it so much or because we were curious to see what it felt like. This would make her feel like a dog and that's not a very good feeling."

Afterward, I answered questions, and left behind *Hair Dance* and another book called *Cornrows* for the children to read. The children and teacher thanked me, and I moved on to the kindergarten classroom to give the same presentation.

Overall, the presentation went well. However, something felt fundamentally wrong. Something akin to being beaten up by the cops and then being asked to come in and train the police department about racial profiling in law enforcement. Or maybe like a Mammy feeling grateful for being treated well, remaining forever loyal to massa and serving as his personal cultural ambassador—his Black pocket dictionary—translating the strange, unusual ways of Black folk…all to calm his fears and satisfy his curiosity.

The experience really fucked with my social justice sensibilities. However, I was still glad I did it. I really believed in the sincerity of the handful of teachers and parents at that school who wanted the institution to change. I had to do it because there were far too many incidents Baby Girl endured for me not to fight back through education. I needed her to see her Mama defending her honor and the honor of all our kin with hair hailing from Africa.

The amount of emotional stamina—the number of smiles and other unnatural things—required to keep one from slapping someone's hand, cussing somebody out, or snatching off kneecaps when faced with a world that repeatedly attempts to strip you and your family of its dignity is enormous. This emotional stamina must be praised for its depth and longevity. Should I be thanked for my patience and mild-mannered approaches to confronting injustice, let also my latent anger be acknowledged and respected.

It was this emotional stamina that I drew from in that classroom. This education was necessary, but it is only one front on which the battle must be fought. There is a difference in approach between a workshop that teaches non-Black children about Black hair and a workshop that instills Black children with pride in their hair and every other aspect of their being. Such education must become widespread to reverse the self-hatred that has already set in. It must remind us of the beauty of our inheritance, gifts from the ancestors that we can proudly reclaim and show off. It must provide a space, an anchor where we can freely celebrate each others' beautiful halos and crowns, and embrace this beauty no matter what space we step into. Here we can sing loudly to Les Nubians' "Afrodance," Lady of Rage's "Afro Puffs," Meklit's "Kemekem (I Like Your Afro)," and "Hold On" by Pharoahe Monch and Erykah Badu.[6] Why hide? There's no shame in letting Africa shine through, free of shackles, no matter where we are in the world. Stay Black.

Blessings always,

Janet

---

[6] Big thanks to my husband, Shawn Taylor, who shared "Afrodance," "Hold On," and "Kemekem (I Like Your Afro)" with me. These songs have filled our home and brought much self-love and self-reflection into our lives.

Letter #4: terror

July 24, 2015

To Black Parents Visiting Earth:

So much has happened in the last month and half. I bounce between wanting to tell you what happened and wanting to tell you how all of it makes me feel. Just when I think starting with how I feel will be easier, the words stop because my feelings are blunted. So I'll start simple…

Throughout June and July, I put gas in my car, did laundry, pulled some weeds, went swimming, took a road trip to LA, made *kik alicha*, *samgyetang*, and raspberry-lemon curd muffins for the first time, drove my daughter to summer camp and art class, went to the movies, ate my favorite ice cream, and my husband and I celebrated our 13th anniversary.

Being with the people I love, doing the things I enjoy, and taking care of things that need to get done bring a sense of stability and contentment to my life. They provide me with something I can look forward to, something to hold on to. They have predictable outcomes: I know when I put gas in my car, it will take me where I need to go; when I cook and bake, I know I will feel happy. To me, the certainty signals normalcy.

But things are not normal for us as a family right now. News of Black people getting killed is not just news. It's worry. It's fear. It's pain.

As if the police killings of unarmed Black people (men, women, and trans folks) over the last decade weren't enough, hearing more about us being beaten, killed, chased out, and imitated during the months of June and July pushed me into a place where I refused to feel. After each new incident, once the numbness subsided, I was scared first and cried later. Anger came but was cut short by a new incident, and again, I didn't want to feel.

That's how the cycle went when I heard news of:

➢ Dajerria Becton being thrown down and pinned to the ground by Cpl. Casebolt at the pool party in McKinney, TX[7]

➢ Dolezal's charade[8]

➢ The murder of Rev./Sen. Clementa Pinckney, Cynthia Hurd, Sharonda Coleman-Singleton, Tywanza Sanders, Susie Jackson, Myra Thompson, Ethel Lee Lance, Rev./Dr. Daniel Simmons, Rev. Depayne Middleton-Doctor in Charleston, SC[9]

➢ The hundreds of thousands of Haitians and Dominicans of Haitian descent in danger of being expelled from Dominican Republic[10]

[7] Lauren Zakalik, "Texas Police Officer in Pool Party Video Identified," *USA Today*, June 9, 2015, http://www.usatoday.com/story/news/nation/2015/06/08/texas-police-officer-reaction-pool-party/28673177/. See also Tom Cleary, "Dajerria Becton: 5 Fast Facts You Need to Know," *Heavy*, June 8, 2015, http://heavy.com/news/2015/06/dajerria-becton-mckinney-texas-black-girl-bikini-name-assaulted-video-photo-interview-friends-eric-casebolt/.
[8] Zeba Blay "Why Comparing Rachel Dolezal to Kaitlyn Jenner is Detrimental to Trans and Racial Progress," *Huffington Post*, June 12, 2015, http://www.huffingtonpost.com/2015/06/12/rachel-dolezal-caitlyn-jenner_n_7569160.html.
[9] Jessica Simeone, Tasneem Nashrulla, Ema O'Connor, and Tamerra Griffin, "These are the Victims of the Charleston Church Shooting," *BuzzFeed News*, June 18, 2015, http://www.buzzfeed.com/jessicasimeone/these-are-the-victims-of-the-charleston-church-shooting#.tf24PjP0E.
[10] Roxanna Altholz and Laurel E. Fletcher, "The Dominican Republic Must Stop Expulsions of Haitians," *New York Times*, July 5, 2015, http://www.nytimes.com/2015/07/06/opinion/the-dominican-republic-must-stop-expulsions-of-haitians.html. See also Leah Libresco, The Dominican

➢ The burning of eight Black churches in ten days throughout the South[11]

➢ Sandra Bland's death while in police custody in Waller County, TX[12]

Nonstop. One after the next. And this is just a sample of events in June and July impacting Black folks.

But, let's back up.

Two days before Dajerria was thrown to the ground, a Black boy around twelve gets his face slammed into the ground in Albany, CA by two white police officers when his skateboard slips out from under him and hits the rear passenger tire of their cop car. My husband witnessed the whole thing and came over to the officers, attempting to explain. One of the officers unsnapped the holster to his pistol, threatened my husband, and then asked him if he "wanted some." Luckily, two other Albany police officers approached, one of whom my husband happened to know. My husband explained to the officer what had just taken place. This officer then released both my husband and the boy.

My husband, our daughter, and I stood in our home that night, crying as we held each other, thankful that Daddy was still alive. My husband and I agreed

Republic's Revocation of Citizenship Creates 200,000 Stateless People, *Five Thirty Eight*, June 17, 2015, http://fivethirtyeight.com/datalab/the-dominican-republics-revocation-of-citizenship-creates-200000-stateless-people/; Esther Yu-Hsi Lee, "Dominican Republic Revokes Citizenship for Haitian Children," *Think Progress*, September 30, 2013, http://thinkprogress.org/immigration/2013/09/30/2693951/dominican-republic-revoke-citizenship/.

[11] Alissa Greenberg, "Another Black Church Burns in the South, the 8th in 10 Days," *Time*, July 1, 2015, http://time.com/3942688/black-church-burning-mount-zion-ame-south-carolina/.

[12] David Montgomery, "Sandra Bland was Threatened with Taser Police Video Shows," *New York Times*, July 21, 2015, http://www.nytimes.com/2015/07/22/us/sandra-bland-was-combative-texas-arrest-report-says.html.

we could not stay here. Though he and I understood that "here" meant this country, we were unclear if there existed a place we could escape to and actually be safe.

Safe. Safe is a funny word. I can feel safe and yet be in serious danger. This is what disturbs me the most about the nine murdered in Charleston. I'm sure they felt safe in Emanuel AME Church during their Bible study meeting. A worship space rightfully should be a congregation's sanctuary, not it's death chamber. I don't like that gap between perception and reality, but it's always there.

Anyways, what's also disturbing is noticing my behavior change little-by-little over the years as I attempt to do things I perceive will make me (or those I care about) safe. For example:

➢ I stopped wearing a hoodie while jogging in my neighborhood.

➢ I keep a close eye on my husband if he goes into a gas station alone just to make sure he is safe.

➢ I ask my husband not to go out alone after dark (not even in our driveway).

➢ I notice myself thinking twice before attending an event with a predominantly Black audience/congregation/etc. in fear that we could be a target of violence.

➢ If organizing an event drawing a Black audience, I think twice about publicly disclosing location/time in the interest of protecting the audience from potential harm.

All these things are done in an attempt to lessen the likelihood that I or the people I care about will become targets of violence—meager, nearly futile exercises in self-preservation that don't guarantee safety when faced with the unpredictable movement of racial hatred.

The violent acts we have witnessed have effectively instilled fear in our Black families, our Black communities. They are terrorist acts. Acts of terrorism gradually twist the minds of its targets, making us search for ways to change our behavior in order to remain safe; truly, the perpetrators and the systems that sustain, support, and protect them need to change.

White supremacy (overt and covert) is building momentum and becoming more brazen. Anti-blackness is alive and well. As more Black folk are killed due to the racist hatred of white people and people of color who pass or don't pass as white (but identify with and embrace white supremacy), the truth that we don't live in a post-racial society becomes loud and clear for those long in denial. At the same time, these incidents inspire and embolden white supremacists to continue to unleash and act upon their insatiable racist rage.

With each week that passes, I wonder what will happen next. *Who will be the next to die? When will they stop killing us?*

Please understand: I don't sit in my livingroom all day, everyday, rocking back and forth, wondering if I might die. I am not crippled by the fear, but I'm certainly stifled by it. The fear lingers in the background while I put gas in my car, do laundry, pull weeds, cook, bake, work, eat, sleep, and pray.

Dear Black parents on Earth, all I can say for now is, at minimum, we need to equip ourselves with self-defense skills as well as negotiation and de-escalation techniques. Of course, these skills are no substitute for the essential reform in legislation, the criminal justice system, and law enforcement needed to ensure that the human value and dignity of African Americans is recognized, respected, and protected in the first place. There's also no guarantee that such skills will save us from being shot in the back or having our house or church set on fire. However, these are skills we can acquire now to maximize our chances of survival in situations where we are unprotected by the authorities—an ugly reality of Black life in the United States.

To Black parents planning to visit Earth, it is not safe for you to come here. Not now.

Sincerely,

Janet

Letter #5: dolls

January 15, 2016

To Black Parents Visiting Earth:

I was sorting through Baby Girl's old dolls and came across Taraji and Wangari. Taraji is a brown-skinned baby doll from Target and Wangari is a brown-skinned Cabbage Patch Kid we received as a gift. My daughter was just a baby when these dolls entered her life, so I took the liberty of giving them African names.

The Target doll was named Taraji which means "hope" or "faith" in Swahili. I can't remember what name was on the Cabbage Patch Kid's birth certificate, but since Daddy had just bought the book *Wangari's Trees of Peace: A True Story from Africa* for Baby Girl, I decided to name the doll after Wangari Maathai, the founder of the Green Belt Movement.

Before our daughter was born, my husband and I were well aware of Kenneth and Mamie Clark's doll experiments from 1939-1940 and Kiri Davis' film *Girl Like Me* from 2007 and knew she was prone to internalizing negative ideas about Blackness that could lead her to choose white dolls over Black dolls.[13] So we decided to take preventative measures and surround her with Black dolls (light- and dark-skinned) at home and away from home.

---

[13] Kenneth Clark and Mamie Clark, "The Development of Consciousness of Self and the Emergence of Racial Identification in Negro Preschool Children," *Bell and Howell Information and Learning Company*, 2000, http://drsmorey.org/bibtex/upload/Clark:Clark:1939.pdf. See also Kenneth Clark and Mamie Clark, "Skin Color As a Factor in Racial Identification of Negro

But, it hasn't been easy. Walking into a toy store and seeing shelves and shelves of white dolls is a given; and the dolls are either babies or ladies— nothing in between. If you do see Black dolls, it's usually Doc McStuffins or the lone Princess Tiana in a sea of nearly all-white Disney princesses, Sasha of the hypersexualized Bratz dolls with no noses, Clawdeen Wolf from Monster High, or more recently, action figures of Finn from *Star Wars: The Force Awakens*. It's rare to find white dolls that aren't princesses in billowy evening gowns or little divas in miniskirts and even rarer to find Black dolls within such a limited selection.

Most of the dolls out there emphasize physical beauty and glamour, the range being so tragically narrow: princess, fashion model, make-up, dresses. Why is physical beauty prioritized as the single dream that doll manufacturers seek to plant into girls' minds? And when the physical beauty and glamour are gone, what's left?

I'm looking for dolls that represent active girls on a mission that doesn't always involve making a fashion statement. As a parent, what are my options? What are my child's options?

Will doll manufacturers sell an image that inspires girls to dream of being inventors, businesswomen, warriors, political leaders, professors, lawyers, doctors…skydivers?! If they do come up with a doll that fits the bill, will it be affordable and widely available…not some limited edition $300 doll I can only find online or in the corner of Bloomingdale's?!

When my husband and I began our search for Black dolls (or apparel with Black images), we discovered how exhausting that shit really was. We started eight years ago. Now we don't even look. We have better luck finding things by accident. And so whenever we come across that one doll or that one T-

Preschool Children," *PsychCentral*, accessed January 10, 2016, http://psychcentral.com/classics/Clark/Skin-color/; Kiri Thomas, "A Girl Like Me," *Media That Matters*, 2007, https://www.youtube.com/watch?v=YWyI77Yh1Gg.

shirt that fits everything we're looking for, we grab it right away because we might not find it again. I advise you to do the same...or create what's missing.

Thankfully, there have been some pleasant surprises, not only in stores, but also at my daughter's daycare and in one particular public play space. I am forever grateful for the help of friends who were on similar quests, Baby Girl's grandparents and godparents who understood the quest, and the caregivers who already knew or demonstrated a willingness to learn about the importance of seeing positive reflections of yourself in the world around you.

So, as I mentioned earlier, Taraji and Wangari were the first two Black dolls in her life. Here are a few snapshots of how other Black dolls became a part of her life:

Daycare
Baby Girl was at the same daycare center from five months to five years old. The director and the majority of the caregivers were African American women. We were surprised to find only white dolls in the infant room. I spoke to the director and Baby Girl's main caregiver about the lack of Black and Brown dolls, and they openly admitted that they never noticed this before. I shared Clarks' research with them and within a couple weeks, there were Black and Brown dolls in the infant room and eventually in the toddler room, as well. Really happy they were so responsive.

Indoor Play Space
From about four months old to about three years old, we brought her to Studio Grow in Berkeley, an indoor play space for children. I was happy to find that in the room where the kids can play make-believe, there were only Black dolls. Though I never asked the managers about this, I had the sense this was a conscious decision. I was comforted by the thought that my child could play in a space where she could see dolls that look like her. I was also comforted by the idea that children of all ethnicities could play with Black dolls and accept this as normal.

Post-Taraji/Wangari Era
After Taraji and Wangari, there were other Black dolls (of various shades) that entered her life and they were:

- ➤ A Doc McStuffins doll bought on Amazon.com; comes with a stethoscope, medical bag, syringe, and tweezers

- ➤ Tons of Black dolls from grandma

- ➤ Dr. Lopez, a female doctor puppet from Puppets on the Pier at Pier 39, San Francisco

- ➤ Botswana, a dark-skinned doll we found at Arts Africains in Emeryville; Baby Girl was inspired to name her Botswana after watching *The No. 1 Ladies' Detective Agency* and also hearing me read *The Great Cake Mystery* at bedtime

- ➤ Imani, a dark-skinned doll made in Palestine that we bought at the Bay Area Anarchist Book Fair in San Francisco

- ➤ Storm, a Funko Pop! Marvel action figure from Cape and Cowl Comics in Oakland; also available at Amazon.com

- ➤ Ruby Rails, a GoldieBlox action figure found in the children's clothing department of Bloomingdale's; comes with parachute, backpack, and tech accessories; also available at Amazon.com

- ➤ Nneka, Wuraola, and Azeezah, purchased on Queensofafricadolls.com, are also a part of our daughter's collection; they are African queens that come with different outfits, Afro hairstyles, accessories, and a pet

As first-time parents, we discovered big and small ways we could instill a love of Blackness and Africanity in our child's heart. We've worked hard to make sure Baby Girl is immersed in positive reflections of herself, as a Black child, as a mixed child, and as a girl. I share our experience and this list of dolls so you know they exist, and you know where to find them.

If you have a child and want to avoid searching all over creation for dolls, then hopefully this letter will save you some time.

Love always,

Janet

LETTER #6: ORLANDO via SANTA MONICA

June 30, 2016

To Black Parents Visiting Earth,

Daydreaming about flaky pastries and green eggs and ham wasn't good enough. I had to go to the source: Huckleberry Café in Santa Monica. After seeing it on the LA episode of *I'll Have What Phil's Having*, I'd been eating there in my head ever since.

So, for our annual Mommy-and-Baby LA road trip, I decided Huckleberry Café would be our first stop. Took only about 5 ½ hours to get there. On the way, we snacked on hashbrowns and blasted *Hamilton* in the car. No need to stop for gas. Just one quick bathroom stop in a town that smelled like cows. The cows didn't spoil our day because school was out and we had fresh pedicures and we couldn't wait to sleep in and wake up just to have fun. And when we arrived, I didn't even have to pay for parking—damn near perfect day.

Huckleberry Café was everything I imagined it to be: long line, friendly faces, tons of pastries, busy kitchen. But the green eggs and ham…can I tell you: eggs sunnyside up with prosciutto on homemade English muffins, pesto drizzled on top, and the whole dish was covered with fresh arugula. You ain't ready!

Baby Girl had their quiche. No other real details for you. It wasn't as good as Daddy's, but she still ate the whole thing…and a brownie she kept looking at while eating the quiche.

Since Mommy's priority was out of the way, I brought her to Third Street Promenade and the Santa Monica Pier. It was a day of saying yes to Baby Girl:

Yes, you can go on the trampoline bungee ride.
Yes, we can go on the bumper cars.
Yes, we can buy a Slurpee.
Yes, you can play in the water…even though we don't have a towel or a change of clothes.

While Baby Girl jumped and flipped on the trampoline bungee ride, I checked my phone and saw the news about the killings in Orlando. I couldn't believe it. I was numb and the carnival rides faded in the background. I didn't tell Baby Girl.

I knew LA Pride was going on that weekend. A friend of mine, Leon, is a DJ at a club in LA, so I texted him to see how he was doing. He was scheduled to do a set at the Latin stage later that night in West Hollywood. Leon just asked me to wish him luck and a safe time at Pride. *Safe. That word again.*

Later that night, I found out that a man, who was planning to go to LA Pride, was arrested in Santa Monica for having assault rifles and explosives in his car. This was only a few hours before we arrived at Huckleberry's.

Baby Girl's time was up on the bungee ride. *Should I tell her? Not tell her? Tell her?*

I didn't tell her.

Bumper cars. Slurpee. Dart game. Bumper cars. Beach. We were exhausted. I still said nothing about Orlando.

We walked back to the car. Baby Girl's shorts were soaking wet and all I could think about was getting her into some warm, dry clothes. We passed by a tall Black woman walking across the street. She was stunning.

"She's beautiful!" I said.
Baby girl asked, "Is that a man or a woman?"
"She's transgender, mama." Silence. I fumbled a bit before I finally found the words I thought would make sense to a presumably straight, cisgender 8-year-old: "Sometimes a person who is born a man may feel more at home living life as a woman. You and I, we would be considered cisgender. That means there is alignment between our biological sex and our gender…that we were both born female; I live my daily life as a woman, and you live your daily life as a girl."[14]
"Oh, ok" she said.

That evening, we had dinner with a dear friend, Fr. Jesse Montes, and watched the Tony Awards. From James Corden dedicating the Tony's to the Orlando victims to Lin Manuel Miranda's acceptance speech and all the commercial interruptions for the 11:00 news, Baby Girl put everything together and started asking questions: "Why would he kill a bunch of people? He didn't even know them. Why does he hate gay people? Why is this world so horrible?" She was overwhelmed. Baby Girl eventually fell asleep in my arms, seeming dissatisfied with the answers Fr. Jesse and I offered her.

The following day we went to USC to visit the different cultural centers on campus: Center for Black Cultural and Student Affairs (CBCSA), Asian Pacific American Students Services (APASS) and El Centro Chicano. Coming out of the elevator, El Centro was the first center we saw, but it was closed. After visiting the other centers, Corliss Bennett-McBride, the director of the CBCSA recommended we go back to El Centro; she knew they were closed earlier because they had a joint memorial with the LGBT Resource

---

[14] At the time, I didn't explain terms like non-binary and genderqueer and how there are people who don't identify as a man or woman, but instead may identify: 1) as both at the same time, 2) with more than two genders, 3) as a third/fourth gender, or 4) with no gender at all. I want to make sure I bring this up in the future.

Center. We went back and sure enough El Centro was open. Baby Girl and I walked in. Two flat screen TVs were on the wall, both broadcasting news updates of the Orlando shooting. The volume was turned down but Baby Girl quickly read the captions and learned that the killer told his wife what he was planning to do. All of us in the room watched. Baby Girl said, "Oh what's that?" I said, "Ok, let's go, you've seen enough of this." I turned to the student at the welcome desk and said, "She's been asking why this world is so horrible." The woman leaned over the desk toward my daughter and said, "Don't worry. When you grow up, you will help to make it a better place."

I have shared similar words with my daughter many times in the past. More than I wish was necessary. However, in this moment, I lacked the conviction that our country could ever change. I was too bitter to be hopeful. But, I was happy that a stranger was able to share with my daughter what I could not.

Your Sister in Spirit,

Janet

LETTER #7: TIME BENDERS
IN A NEW ERA

December 16, 2016

To Black Parents Visiting Earth:

I have spent nearly 20 years of my life doing social justice work, fighting alongside others to dismantle various systems of oppression. Most of this work has been done in the classroom and some of it done as a writer.

Throughout that time, I have been accused of brainwashing. Accused of religious malpractice. Reverse racism. I have been accused of being too sensitive, too radical, too soft, too angry, and too biased—and if all this were actually true, then I'd say accomplishing this all at the same time was quite impressive. Such charges came from either people of color unready to change or white people who thought they'd changed enough. Even though I can count these moments on one hand, the wounds left behind are real and have required some time to heal.

In spite of all this, I'm happy to say that overall, my commitment to this work has been received with far more openness than resistance. I have been encouraged by my students' attentiveness and eagerness to engage with material that may cause thoughts and feelings to emerge that they didn't know were there. It's beautiful to see a growing desire amongst students to feel a greater connection to their ancestors, to the land, to each other, and to their future.

I am honored to have students tell me how much my classes have meant to them; how they are emotionally stronger, more inspired to accomplish their goals; how they are ready to love across boundaries, seeing difference as something to celebrate as opposed to seeing it as a threat; how they have more tools, more language with which to think critically about power structures; how they can live freer, healthier lives and be catalysts for loving transformation with all those they encounter in their own professional and personal lives.

There are many of us educators who've worked hard over the decades to share Truth(s) with our students.[15] We have been moved to tears by what can be unearthed in the classroom. We are not saviors. We are revealers of the beauty that already lies within our students.

I am fortunate enough to belong to an unofficial network of educators who stand in and out of classrooms with a book in one hand and not-much-time in the other, ready to receive these beautiful minds and hearts with open arms. We are time benders of a sort. As time benders, we work miracles in the world of academia (though we can also be found in other fields) where every bit of work gets squeezed out of us unless we say no. We manage to do the impossible in an unreasonably short amount of time. We are aware of the breadth and depth of material we must cover in 18-, 15-, 10- or sometimes 8-week sessions and wonder how we will do it all and still make it meaningful for our students. How do we teach so that they come out on the other side changed forever, never once feeling rushed?

Time benders absorb the rush and are ever aware of the Theodore Parker-inspired Martin Luther King, Jr. quote, "The arc of the moral universe is long,

---

[15] It took me awhile to articulate my post-election reflections. Reading the honest words of Dawn Mabalon, Kevin Nadal, E.J.R. David, and Gregg Popovich gave me the courage to empty these thoughts onto paper.

but it bends toward justice."[16] We absorb the speed and the volume and slow down time for our students. We make time expand and contract to fit the shape of the untold narrative…to make room for the untold narrative. Time benders spare the student the feeling of overwhelm by carrying the burden for them; this way they are free to immerse themselves in the newness of the experience. Time benders create microcosms of understanding and belonging in the classroom, bearing witness to a clarity, justice, and unity some thought could only be achieved centuries from now. In this environment, students learn from teacher, teacher learns from student, and student learns from student. All learn what this world feels like, sounds like, tastes like…and realize that that world can be created today. And with that realization, we expand this circle of understanding far beyond the four walls of their inception and replicate that feeling of connectedness and belonging over and over again.

This is what many of us social justice educators attempt to do. This is what I try to do. I may not always be successful, but when I am, the class and I know it.

I won't lie. It's exhausting. It's hard work. It may not always turn out the way I want it to. But when it does (or when it's better than what I envisioned), the rewards are undeniable.

Overall, in the classroom, I see things moving forward.

As far as the national arena, though we still have a long way to go (especially considering the ongoing state-sanctioned violence against Black and Brown people, legislation allowing discrimination of LGBTQ people on the basis of religious freedom, the inhumane treatment of undocumented immigrants, sexual harassment and assault, mass shootings, corporate greed, and more), I was beginning to feel like our country was making some good steps in the right direction throughout Obama's eight years as the President of the United

---

[16] Gary O'Toole, "The Arc of the Moral Universe is Long, But It Bends Toward Justice," *The Quote Investigator,* November, 15, 2012, http://quoteinvestigator.com/2012/11/15/arc-of-universe/.

States. Seeing these changes under his administration signaled we were
making moves toward greater justice and inclusion. Here are some listed
below:

> American Recovery Reinvestment Act of 2009
> Affordable Care Act of 2010
> Dodd-Frank Act of 2010
> Sotomayor becomes Supreme Court justice[17]
> Supreme Court ruling in favor of marriage equality[18]
> Executive actions like:
  o Deferred Action for Childhood Arrivals (DACA)
  o Deferred Action for Parents of Americans and Lawful
    Permanent Residents (DAPA)[19]
> Executive orders like:
  o White House Initiative for Educational Excellence for
    African Americans
  o White House Initiative on American Indian and Alaska
    Native Education
  o White House Initiative for Educational Excellence for
    Hispanics
  o White House Initiative on Asian Americans and Pacific
    Islanders

---

[17] Charlie Savage, "Sotomayor Confirmed by Senate, 68-31," *The New York Times*,
August 6, 2009,
http://www.nytimes.com/2009/08/07/us/politics/07confirm.html.
[18] Adam Liptak, "Supreme Court Ruling Makes Same-Sex Marriage a Right
Nationwide," *The New York Times*, June 26, 2015,
http://www.nytimes.com/2015/06/27/us/supreme-court-same-sex-
marriage.html.
[19] Melanie Garunay, "Live Updates: President Obama on the Supreme Court
Ruling on Immigration Reform," *The White House: President Obama*, June 23, 2016,
https://obamawhitehouse.archives.gov/blog/2016/06/23/president-obama-
supreme-court-ruling-immigration-reform. See also Muzaffar Chishti and Faye
Hipsman, "Supreme Court DAPA Ruling a Blow to Obama Administration, Moves
Immigration Back to Political Realm," *Migration Policy Institute*, June 29, 2016,
http://www.migrationpolicy.org/article/supreme-court-dapa-ruling-blow-obama-
administration-moves-immigration-back-political-realm.

- ➤ White House Minority Mental Health Summit
- ➤ White House Council on Women and Girls
- ➤ White House Celebrations of Filipino American History Month (the first in 2015)
- ➤ Department of Justice's investigation of the Baltimore Police Department[20]
- ➤ Recent decision to stop Dakota Access Pipeline construction (and examine alternative routes for the pipeline)[21]

As a country, these were significant steps forward.[22] Room for improvement? Certainly. But, in all my years of teaching, it was during these eight under Obama that I noticed more alignment between the time bending going on in my microcosm and the time bending happening on a national scale.

So, when Trump won the presidential election, I felt betrayed, like my country slapped me in the face. Even considering that Clinton won the popular vote, I didn't feel too much better because there were still 62,206,395 people out there who voted for Trump in comparison to 64,223,958 who voted for Clinton.[23] That's still close to half the voters who favored Trump.

---

[20] "Justice Department Announces Findings of Investigation into Baltimore Police Department," *The U.S. Department of Justice*, accessed December 7, 2016, https://www.justice.gov/opa/pr/justice-department-announces-findings-investigation-baltimore-police-department.

[21] "Army Will Not Grant Easement for Dakota Access Pipeline Crossing," *U.S. Army*, accessed December 7, 2016, https://www.army.mil/article/179095/army_will_not_grant_easement_for_dakota_access_pipeline_crossing.

[22] It is also important to note that colleagues and friends like Vangie Buell, Mel Orpilla, Joan May Cordova, Dorothy Cordova, Dawn Mabalon, Allyson Tintiangco-Cubales, Farzana Nayani, Frank Harris III, J. Luke Wood, Kevin Nadal, and E.J.R. David had participated in events associated with some of the White House Initiatives above. Big thanks to all of you who chimed in and shared the specific names of those events. Your work as time benders is priceless.

[23] Gabriel Debenedetti, Kyle Cheney, and Nolan McCaskill, "Clinton's Lead in the Popular Vote Surpasses 2 Million," *Politico*, November 26, 2016, http://www.politico.com/story/2016/11/clinton-lead-popular-vote-2016-231790.

My initial thought was why should I give so much of myself to a country that hates me, the people I love, and the people I fight alongside with. Why should I have my tax dollars go to a country that allows a sexist, Islamophobic, KKK-endorsed racist—someone who joins the ranks of those thinking #AllLivesMatter is an enlightened response to #BlackLivesMatter, who wants to build a wall at U.S./Mexico border to stop illegal immigration and thinks climate change is a hoax made up by China—become the President of the United States? How can Trump voters turn a blind eye to all of this and actually believe that this billionaire—sharply criticized for his business practices—is anti-establishment and could bring about economic development and equality?[24] What will other countries think of us knowing that we elected an ignorant beacon of hate to represent our nation? How embarrassing! And how incredibly dangerous!

All of this was jumbled up in my system and amounted to a rock at the pit of my stomach and intermittent tears. I didn't have the words immediately; I just felt sick. It's not like I was completely surprised; you remember from my 4th letter to you on terror, I warned you that white supremacy was building momentum and becoming more brazen. But even though I've seen the oppression this country is capable of—the very foundation on which it was built—and knew the hatred was always lurking out there, I still found Trump's win painful and alarming.

I knew Trump would damage our country, but I first feared his supporters. I was afraid this victory would grant them permission to unapologetically release their hatred, becoming more open than they already were.

At 11:54pm on election day, I posted this on Facebook:

> Those Muslim-hating, xenophobic, racist, sexist, homophobic **** have
> been hating in the privacy of their homes and local neighborhoods. Many

---

[24] Marlow Stern, "Mark Cuban Rips Trump's $916M in Losses 'How the Fuck Do You Do That?'" *The Daily Beast*, October 7, 2016, http://www.thedailybeast.com/articles/2016/10/08/mark-cuban-rips-trump-s-916m-in-losses-how-the-f-ck-do-you-do-that.html.

not even in private...especially over the past few years. Anyways, the hidden ones have been strategic and stealthy...still getting prepared behind closed doors. Now they don't have to hide. Trump is their release. And I fear this victory for them will make it open season for POC, LGBT, immigrant, Muslim, women, and all at the intersections. The violence that will get unleashed...God...I don't even want to think about it. And somehow, somehow I will have to have a conversation with my daughter and my students that gives them some desire to press on. I hope I have the words tomorrow.

Later that night and early the next morning, I urged friends, family, community members to be careful and vigilant. I was scared for them. I was scared for us.

I wish I was wrong, but sure enough, open season began. By the time Friday November 11th came around, there were 201 election-related hate incidents nationwide.[25] By the following Monday on November 14th, it jumped to 437.[26] Within ten days after the election, there were 701 incidents.[27]

But before Day 10, there was Day 1 for my daughter...

*

---

[25] Hatewatch Staff, "Over 200 Incidents of Hateful Harassment and Intimidation Since Election Day," *The Southern Poverty Law Center*, November 11, 2016, https://www.splcenter.org/hatewatch/2016/11/11/over-200-incidents-hateful-harassment-and-intimidation-election-day.

[26] Jennifer Hansler, "Over 400 reports of Hateful Harrassment and Intimidation Post-Election, SPLC Says," *ABC News*, November 15, 2016, http://abcnews.go.com/Politics/200-reports-hateful-harassment-intimidation-post-election-splc/story?id=43491050.

[27] Hatewatch Staff, "Update: Incidents of Hateful Harassment Since Election Day Now Number 701," *The Southern Poverty Law Center*, November 18, 2016, https://www.splcenter.org/hatewatch/2016/11/18/update-incidents-hateful-harassment-election-day-now-number-701.

While Baby Girl was in karate class, I voted and then picked her up. We discussed worries, possible outcomes, and her suggestion to buy a house in Ethiopia. We watched the votes come in on PBS, then she took a break while my husband and I watched the election results. Before going to bed, Baby Girl asked who won. My husband and I told her in disappointment that Trump won. She dropped her head, her body slumped over, and she walked to her room. She quietly curled up in bed, covered her face, but didn't cry. I pulled the covers over her.

She woke up around midnight, "So who is the president?" she asked. She knew, but we told her again.

The following morning, 7:00 a.m., she woke up and asked Daddy, "Is Trump president?"

"Yes, but not now Baby. Obama is still our president until January," my husband said.

That morning, as we walked to the school playground, I tried to encourage her and told her, "We don't want you to worry...you come from a family who fights for justice." It sounded real good at the time. Almost genuine.

Some part of me believed this, or at least wanted to. Despite my own fears, I didn't want her to worry. After all, she's only 8 right? And 8-year-olds shouldn't have to worry about whether or not they're going to be killed, stomped on, have their families torn apart, or have their healthcare taken away. Despite my ideas of what should and should-not-be, the reality was this: the negligence, apathy, misguided and willful ignorance, hatred of government leaders all become the worry of grown-ups and—since children can sense everything—they become the worry of our children too.

I don't remember anything else I said that morning. I don't believe I gave her any real practical tools to get her through the day. No other words. I gave her a hug and a kiss like I do every morning. And perhaps these were better than words anyway.

Later that day, Baby Girl joined hands with a small group of 3rd graders in her class and formed a circle. The election of Trump was their reason. They prayed, cried, and comforted each other.

Baby Girl just happened to mention this at dinner the following night. When I heard this, shock and sadness hit me first before pride. I was crushed that our babies felt the weight of our country's unrest and needed to console each other. Though I was moved by the sweet wisdom of these children, I didn't want this life for them. I didn't want this for my daughter.

*

Baby Girl was so excited to have a brand new suitcase for our trip to Universal Studios. As soon as we bought it, she started packing right away. We'd been planning this trip for months and were ready to leave the weekend after the election. We almost didn't go because we knew we would be passing through Trump territory and were worried about what might happen to us. We went anyway because, as a family, we made a commitment to being better at welcoming abundance into our lives. Translation: we needed to do more fun things together to break up the monotony of the work-school-eat-sleep routine. And, we wanted to keep our promise to Baby Girl.

To safeguard against potential attack, I kept a kali stick near the driver's seat and pepper spray in the door. I made sure my husband also had a kali stick on the passenger side. I gave Baby Girl the other pepper spray, showed her how to use it, and asked her to keep it in her purse just in case.

On the way there and back, I wanted to avoid making unnecessary stops. It made me wish we had a version of *The Green Book* for the 21st century to tell us what restaurants, gas stations, etc. were safe for Black folk.[28]

---

[28] "The Negro Motorist Green Book: 1940," *The New York Public Library Digital Collections*, accessed December 7, 2016, http://digitalcollections.nypl.org/items/dc858e50-83d3-0132-2266-58d385a7b928#/?uuid=dcca52c0-83d3-0132-cdb8-58d385a7b928.

While we were away, we had fun. We spent time with good people. We ate and laughed. And we never had to use the kali sticks or the pepper spray.

By the time we returned to the Bay Area, the hate incidents were rapidly approaching 400 and Trump selects Priebus—someone who claims heterosexual couples are better parents for children compared to same-sex couples—as his chief of staff. He also selects Bannon—alt-right, white supremacist—as his chief strategist.[29] By Friday, November 18th, hate incidents were up to 700 and Sessions—a man considered too racist to be a federal judge in 1986, and someone who doesn't think the act of grabbing-women-by-the-pussy would be sexual assault—is named attorney general.[30] And let's not forget the VP-elect is Pence (proponent of conversion therapy).[31]

Meanwhile, that Friday morning after breakfast, Daddy gave Baby Girl quick lessons on how to poke someone's eyes out if they tried to grab her.

This is our reality.

---

[29] Lauren Carroll, "GOP Chair Wrongly Claims Facts Show Children Do Better With Straight Parents," *Politifact*, July 17, 2016, http://www.politifact.com/truth-o-meter/statements/2016/jul/17/reince-priebus/gop-chair-wrongly-claims-facts-show-children-do-be/. See also The Editorial Board, "Steve 'Turn On the Hate' Bannon, in the White House," *The New York Times*, November 15, 2016, http://www.nytimes.com/2016/11/15/opinion/turn-on-the-hate-steve-bannon-at-the-white-house.html.

[30] Lena Williams, "Senate Panel Hands Reagan First Defeat on Nominee for Judgeship," *The New York Times*, June 6, 1986, http://www.nytimes.com/1986/06/06/us/senate-panel-hands-reagan-first-defeat-on-nominee-for-judgeship.html. See also Laura Bassett, "GOP Senator Says Grabbing a Woman's Genitals is not Sexual Assault," *The Huffington Post*, October 10, 2016, http://www.huffingtonpost.com/entry/jeff-sessions-trump-sexual-assault_us_57fbb902e4b068ecb5e06988.

[31] Chris Nichols, "Pence's Support for Conversion Therapy Not a Settled Matter," *Politifact*, December 2, 2016, http://www.politifact.com/california/statements/2016/dec/02/gavin-newsom/pences-support-conversion-therapy-not-settled-matt/.

White supremacists, homophobes, and misogynists in the White House.

Hate incidents in full effect.

Babies praying and learning to defend themselves.

In short, it's fucking looney-tunes down here.

As Trump is elected as president and he selects his cabinet members, we stare at the perfect green light bringing white supremacy, homophobia, transphobia, misogyny, and every -ism there is, out of the shadows and straight into positions of power to control our country.

This is no set back.[32] A setback suggests that with a few minor corrective measures, we can get back on course. This feels like irrevocable regression.

I bounce between being strong and feeling defeated. I know I have family and students who rely on me to be a source of hope and guidance. I try to stay steady enough to be that source. But when I take stock of my true emotions, my disgust with this country is strong. I am angry and deeply disappointed. Can't say I ever had complete faith in this country and its systems, but what little faith I had, I lost on election day. I fear for my safety, and the safety of my friends and family. Part of me sees no way through this and urges me to make a family exit plan: pack our bags, get the emergency fund and emergency packs together, polish up the martial arts, digital security, and situational awareness skills, get the passports ready, and figure out which country will be our new home.[33] The other part of me will still do most of

---

[32] The original line here was, "Don't call it a setback. They been here for years," a nod to LL Cool J. I removed it because I didn't want to defile LL's lyrics in making reference to white supremacy and this election debacle. Decided to put it in a footnote instead because I was cracking up thinking about how "Mama Said Knock You Out" was in my head while writing this piece.

[33] Lexi Alexander, "A Guide on Situational Awareness: How to Survive in Hostile Environments," *Muslim Girl*, November 19, 2016, http://muslimgirl.com/33895/guide-situational-awareness-survive-hostile-environments/.

the above but not flee. For as long as I remain in this country, I'll continue to resist and call forth the time bender in me and somehow, given the inevitabilities of the Trump administration, not become hopeless. (Not sure how possible this is, but we'll see.) This part of me refuses to let hopelessness consume me because I've watched how this kills people and the ones they love. Hopelessness is just as lethal as a bomb; the only difference is that hopelessness kills gradually and creeps softly.

To combat this hopelessness, I will carve out a space within me that is completely free, completely belongs to me. It cannot be owned, it cannot be sold, it cannot be stolen. I have learned this from my ancestors.

Please do the same. And when you do, let this space be the way you say <u>thank you to yourself</u> for pressing on.

I know in my 4th letter, I told you not to come. Things are not much different from then. In fact, they are about to get worse. But instead of telling you not to come, I will say this: if you do come to the U.S., know what you're getting into and know there have been thousands marching in major cities across the country protesting Trump's election. There are countless other forms of resistance people are engaged in. Find these people.

I hope you are time benders because we need them now more than ever.

I'm not sure if I'll be here to greet you. But perhaps some other time benders will.

With all my love,

Janet

LETTER #8: LEGACY

November 7, 2017

To Black Parents Visiting Earth,

When I was little, I grew up in Lancaster, CA. Da'y was a construction worker. Mama worked on an onion farm.[34] By the time Da'y became too senile to work, Mama enrolled in a clerical training program, hoping to get a job as a secretary. Mama and I picked cans in the park on weekends. Money from the cans and Da'y's Social Security checks were our only sources of income during those years right before Mama passed.

I knew we were poor. Mama and Da'y argued about money all the time. They found ways to stretch a dollar at Grocery Warehouse, Pic 'n' Save, and Kmart; Mama used coupons every chance she could get. Going out to eat was rare: McDonalds was a treat; Sizzler, a dream.

Sometimes, we went to a food bank for a free bag of groceries. I loved going there because we got food we normally couldn't buy—Yoplait, Entenmann's donuts, Count Chocula cereal. Sometimes the food was expired, but it really didn't matter; as a kid, it was still special.

All my parents' worries and wants went up in flames the day our house burned down. Their cries made me think there was no way out when you're poor.

---

[34] D'ay is short for Daddy.

But they lived and cried and lived some more. Judging from how Mama signed me up for tap dancing, swimming, diving, and roller skating lessons, you'd think she saw me as their way out. I don't think my parents ever meant for me to help pay the bills or help them get rich. But I think they needed to know there was a reason to go on; that yes, they were poor, but maybe their child could have a better life.

Though, I'm no professional in any of these things, being so involved in different activities (which eventually led to band, track, B-boy/B-girl battles, spelling bees, and speech contests) all taught me discipline and persistence. I learned that with regular practice, I could watch my skills improve. Making progress motivated me to excel in everything I did. As I excelled in multiple areas, I learned I had options.

When it came to travel, my most memorable experiences were with Mama. We went to Santa Monica or sometimes on city-run bus trips to Magic Mountain or to The Forum to see the Harlem Globetrotters and ice skating exhibitions with Debbie Thomas, Katerina Witt, and Brian Boitano. Mama used her savings to send me to Vancouver and Washington D.C. with the California Junior Scholastic Federation. No matter how little we had, she found a way for me…for us, to see places beyond my hometown…and to have fun.

Da'y took us on road trips up north to Delano, Fresno, and Marysville. We did this for many summers until once he forgot the way and stood by the roadside crying, waving a white handkerchief for someone to help us with directions. I stored that last trip away in my memory to get old in private. I prefer to remember when he was strong.

Da'y worked hard, constructing buildings, roads, tunnels. Between jobs, he went to the union hall at 5:30/6:00 a.m. to be ready for roll call; each time workers heard their names, they moved closer to the top of the list, increasing their chances of getting work. Other times, Da'y spent weeks away, looking for construction work in Marysville.

Da'y's piggyback rides, bedtime kisses, million-dollar smile—that's what I remember most…and I can't forget those grape jelly sandwiches leftover from his lunch. (The best!) At home, I can still hear him saying to Mama, "Gimme some sugar," and Mama saying, "Gimme some of that brown sugar." We laughed and laughed. D'ay's smile at home was the same one I saw in public as he talked to every stranger and friend he ran into.

Though my parents never gave me explicit pep talks about success or reaching my dreams, the ultimate messages I received were these:

> ➤ From Mama: *There's nothing you can't do. There's no limit to where you can go or who you can meet.*
> ➤ From Da'y: *Work hard, give love, be friendly.*

I often wondered how a poor family could have the money for all these lessons and trips. The answer: they saved. Even though my family had very little, they found ways to create memorable experiences. They loved me. Mama, in particular, was conscientious about saving for my personal growth and investing in my ability to dream. I was the reason they saved. I was their priority.

*

I know they tried their best saving for my future. This was clear a couple months before I turned 16. Mama died, Da'y was placed in a nursing home, and I found myself digging through their files. I stumbled upon some bank passbooks for joint accounts in our names, as well as a $200 bond Mama bought for me. It wasn't much, but it was plenty for a scared 15-year-old.

Despite their poverty, they left behind riches I can only thank them for in my prayers. The sacrifices they made, the money, the time, the energy—it was all for me. And I walk with a disciplined, resilient, happy heart because of them. I learned there was no limit to what I could accomplish; I learned that I always have options; I learned friendliness and gratitude. When some parents leave their children houses, family heirlooms, and a million's worth in savings,

Mama and Da'y left me love and priceless life lessons. And since they left behind good, I know how to seek out good.

They may not have high-rises and scholarship foundations in their names, but they left many marks on the world: their daily work, their intimate relationships, the risks they took. The evidence lay imprinted on the hearts of those they touched and the hard work deemed disposable by the masses. This was a major part of their legacy that I hope to carry on.

I think another part of their legacy was me. This sounds cocky whether I say it out loud or read it to myself, but it is only in retrospect—particularly after my husband pointed out how Mama recorded every detail of my life, keeping everything from my perfect attendance awards, good citizenship certificates, and swimming badges to labeling all photos of me and every trophy and plaque with date, age, and location—that this began to seem like the case.

For so many of us people of color—descendants of enslaved Africans, native peoples, immigrants/descendants of immigrants, refugees, first-generation college students, and the intersections thereof—our parents view us as their legacy. This so often fuels their efforts to empty all their hopes and dreams into us. As their children, this can be both burden and blessing, carrying enormous responsibility. Together, our very bodies and the cultural capital that resides within are the legacies our parents leave behind.

Mama showed me the power of having options. Da'y showed me the power of laughter and friendliness. Together, they showed me the importance of building relationships. In return, may I share these lessons with my daughter, keeping their memories alive, speaking fondly of the love they modeled.

*

I want Baby Girl to believe what Mama taught me: there is nothing you can't do. Without this belief, all my baby's efforts will easily collapse.

Belief in being capable of anything can lead to having access to countless options. I want to spare my daughter the ways I struggled, worried, and felt trapped financially. I want her to have the monetary means to gain access to a wide variety of fulfilling experiences—experiences that bring her joy and expand her spheres of influence. To do this, I must continue to learn how to manage my money and build wealth so I can share what I learn with her.

Growing up, I knew it was important to save and not overspend, but that was the extent of my financial literacy. I didn't know how to budget my money or what percentage of my income I should save each month. I never knew how lethal and burdensome credit cards could be; never heard of a credit score because it wasn't introduced until 1989, the year Mama died. Never learned much about investing: I knew about savings and checking accounts, but not brokerage accounts; I'd heard of Medi-Cal share of cost, but not shares of stock; I knew the risk involved when buying lotto and lottery tickets, but never knew about assessing my risk tolerance when it came to investing money.

My vocabulary began to expand in college when I first learned about mutual funds at a National Society of Black Engineers conference. Later, I was exposed to how both earned and passive income lead to financial freedom and building wealth. After I landed my first full-time job, I learned about 401(k)s, 403(b)s, and Roth IRAs and how I could plan for retirement.

I'm still learning and have a long way to go, but now I'm much smarter with my money. Luckily my financial literacy kicked in just in time to prepare for my child's future and share crucial lessons with her about money management and building wealth.

Baby Girl's official lessons in financial literacy began when she was 7. I was listening to an interview that Chris Hogan, author of *Retire Inspired*, did with *Success Magazine* and he spoke about teaching his sons to divide up their money into three categories: save, spend, and give.[35] I had Baby Girl label three Mason jars with these categories. For every $3 she earned, a dollar went into each jar. She developed the habit of putting money into each of these jars; with practice, this will become automatic. As she gets older, she will realize that she is saving 33.33% of her income, setting aside 33.33% to give to others (i.e. to the homeless, birthday gifts, charities, etc.), and has 33.33% of her earnings to spend.

Other lessons from Chris Hogan I strongly recommend practicing with (or starting for) your children are the following:

> "Tell a want it needs to wait."
> Doing chores is work. Instead of "getting an allowance" for doing chores, use the phrase "earning commission"; this language shifts the mentality from being entitled to money to earning money
> Use the EveryDollar app to help create a budget (or "cash flow plan")
> Start a 529 or ESA for your child's education savings
> Begin estate planning

I also learned very quickly that I need to teach Baby Girl how to create lists when it comes to spending. I get anxious whenever we're in a store and Baby Girl says, "Ooo, Mama look!" because I know what's sure to follow is "Can we get it?" It gets worse around the holidays. The child knows exactly what she wants; been that way ever since she was a baby. I love this about her, and I know it will serve her well throughout her adolescence and adulthood (since ambivalence often creates too much room for others to define your wants for you). However, within this context, she needs to pay attention to her collective wants and needs. To avoid going broke and to prevent her from thinking it's okay to impulse-buy, I taught her to create a list of things she wants (along with the cost) and rank them according to urgency (i.e. how

---

[35] "Chris Hogan on Want vs. Need," September 8, 2015, in SUCCESS Talks Collection, produced by *SUCCESS Magazine*, podcast, MP3 audio, 22:58, accessed November 7, 2017, www.success.com/podcast/chris-hogan-on-want-vs-need.

badly she wants the item, how soon she wants it). She can save her money and buy what she wants only if it's on her list. Essentially, she is learning how to prioritize and monitor her spending habits—a practice aligned with Hogan's advice to, "Tell a want it needs to wait."

As far as investing, we haven't gotten that far yet. When we do, I'll begin with *The Mint* and *The Stock Market Game*. *The Mint* teaches children simple lessons about investing which includes the idea of dividing your earnings into four categories as opposed to three: save, spend, give, and invest.[36] *The Stock Market Game* offers classroom, afterschool program, and homeschool resources teaching students the fundamentals of investing.[37]

While on this track of building wealth, I have to model good spending and saving habits. And most certainly, make gratitude central to our everyday lives. Sometimes I find myself daydreaming about what I want and what I could have and how much bigger and better it would be. This makes it real easy to lose sight of the good things I have right now. I figure if I don't know how to appreciate the blessings I have now, how will I be able to receive and fully appreciate the blessings I will have in the future, big or small?

*

I know for some of us, talking about building wealth is uncomfortable because we're taught to despise money. Folks might hear things like:

- ➢ Money will change you.
- ➢ Money makes you greedy.
- ➢ Money is the root of all evil.
- ➢ Wealthy people can't be trusted.
- ➢ Capitalism won't save you.

---

[36] "What is the Stock Market?" *The Mint*, accessed November 7, 2017, http://www.themint.org/kids/what-is-the-stock-market.html.

[37] "The Stock Market Game," *SIFMA Foundation*, accessed November 7, 2017, www.stockmarketgame.org/expparent.html#popup-video-1.

When you encounter some of these folks, ask them about their retirement plan. If they have kids, ask them how much they've saved for their child's future. You'll discover that as much as they may wish they had more money, the ideas above end up being toxic and sabotage their ability to make more money. Our feelings and attitudes toward money have an impact on our ability to build wealth, whether it be earned or passive income.

Personally, I don't see money as evil. This doesn't mean I salivate at the sight of cash. And this doesn't mean I see myself as better than anyone else. This doesn't make me naïve enough to believe capitalism is beyond critique.[38] I have no delusions about capitalism saving me or the collective spirit of Black folk. However, as long as capitalism is this country's economic system, financial literacy is crucial to effectively navigate this system and not get consumed by it. Eliminating personal debt and building wealth is vital. Monetary wealth is not the be-all, end-all, for sure. But, greater wealth can lead to more options to choose from. And this wealth has the potential to grow with each generation. It gives us the ability to support the people, the organizations, the movements we believe in. Chris Hogan explains it beautifully when he says:

> Money is a tool. Money allows us to be able to do the things for the people that we love the most. It allows us to give and impact charities and worthwhile organizations all across the world. It is an incredible tool, put in the right hands of people with the right hearts…it's something you've been entrusted with to manage well…whether we are running our own business or whether we're running our household…I want to make sure that I'm managing this to the best of my ability. It's the love of money that is the root of all evil. Money itself is not an evil thing.[39]

---

[38] Emma Roller, "How the U.S. Government locked Black Americans Out of Attaining the American Dream," *Splinter News*, October 11, 2017, https://splinternews.com/how-the-u-s-government-locked-black-americans-out-of-a-1819221197.

[39] "Chris Hogan on Want vs. Need," September 8, 2015, in SUCCESS Talks Collection, produced by *SUCCESS Magazine*, podcast, MP3 audio, 22:58, accessed November 7, 2017, https://www.success.com/podcast/chris-hogan-on-want-vs-need.

I don't ever want Baby Girl to cry like my parents and I did, worrying about not having enough money. I want her mind to immediately go to "YES"— yes, I can afford to travel; yes, I can go to the college of my choice; yes, I can afford to buy a reliable car...and afford the repairs; yes, I can buy a home; yes, I have what it takes to land a position that offers medical benefits (including vision and dental) so I don't have to pay out-of-pocket; yes, I can afford to buy acres of land and build on my own property; yes, I can create a collective which will buy an entire block (or two or three) before developers pile in to gentrify the neighborhood;[40] yes, I'll buy an SRO so residents don't have to worry about becoming homeless; yes, I have enough to build affordable housing for others; yes, I can start my own school, clinic, community center; yes, I have the educational and professional background to become a policymaker or lawmaker, granting me access to the table to make decisions that impact underrepresented and underserved communities; yes, I can create institutions that provide the working class poor with access to greater options in life (i.e. access to medical care, childcare, education, homeownership, investments, etc.); yes, I can afford to bail protesters out of jail; yes, I can afford an attorney when someone or some institution violates my civil rights; yes, I can help my friends and family if they're suffering financially; yes, I can make a donation to a cause I believe in; yes, I can establish a grantmaking network; yes, I can afford to create a scholarship fund for students who want to go to college but can't afford it; yes, I can leave an abusive relationship or a hostile work environment without worrying if I can sustain myself financially. These are the options I'm talking about—options that offer us greater autonomy and control.

And such aspirations are not new to us as a people. At bedtime, I remind my daughter of our own history of entrepreneurs:

> ➤ Broteer Furro (eldest son of a prince, known later by his slave name, Venture Smith) bought his freedom for 71 pounds and two shillings

---

[40] "Buy the Block," accessed November 7, 2017, www.buytheblock.com.

and bought his wife and children out of slavery; eventually he owned over 100 acres of land in Connecticut.[41]

➢ Clara Brown, who outlived two of her slaveowners, was freed in her fifties and eventually owned a laundry business and invested in real estate.[42]

➢ Maggie Lena Walker, owner of the Saint Luke Penny Savings Bank which survived October 1929 stock market crash by merging with two other black-owned banks to become the Consolidated Bank and Trust.[43]

➢ O.W. Gurley who bought 40 acres of land in 1906; he sold that land to other African Americans, creating what became known as Black Wall Street, the Greenwood District of Tulsa, OK.[44]

Today, much respect to entrepreneurs, artists, athletes, and organizers like:

➢ Tristan Walker, CEO of Walker and Company Brands and most known for Bevel, a shaving kit subscription service for men of color; Walker is also the cofounder and chairman of Code 2040, a nonprofit that helps Black and Latino students get jobs with major technology companies[45]

---

[41] Tonya Bolden, *Pathfinders: The Journeys of 16 Extraordinary Black Souls* (New York: Abrams Books for Young Readers, 2017), 5-9.
[42] Ibid, 41-45.
[43] Ibid, 53-57.
[44] "O.W. Gurley: The Visionary Builder," Black Wall Street USA, accessed November 7, 2017, www.blackwallstreet.org/owgurly. See also Kimberly Fain, "The Devastation of Black Wall Street," *JSTOR*, July 5, 2017, https://daily.jstor.org/the-devastation-of-black-wall-street/.
[45] Victor Luckerson, "Meet the Silicon Valley CEO Opening Doors for People of Color," *Time*, March 14, 2016, http://time.com/4254855/tristan-walker-company-brands-bevel/.

➢ Lisa Price, founder/CEO of Carol's Daughter, Black haircare line; Price has donated to the Arthur Ashe Foundation, Hale House, and the September 11th Fund; she is also a board member of the Foundation for the Advancement of Women Now[46]

➢ Morgan DeBaun and Aaron Samuels, cofounders of Blavity, Inc., a technology and multimedia company supporting the interests and innovations of Black millennials across the African diaspora[47]

➢ Naa Hammond, program officer of Groundswell Fund, the largest national funder of the reproductive justice movement in the U.S.; prior to this, Hammond worked in research and communications for Funders for LGBT Issues[48]

➢ Big Freedia, the queen of Bounce music, whose charitable work raised funds for AIDS awareness and victims of Hurricane Harvey[49]

---

[46] "Lisa Price," *The History Makers*, accessed November 7, 2017, www.thehistorymakers.org/biography/lisa-price-41. See also "Lisa Price," *The Huffington Post*, accessed November 7, 2017, https://www.huffingtonpost.com/author/lisa-price.

[47] Julian Mitchell, "Meet Morgan DeBaun: The Blavity Founder Bridging the Gap Between Content and Tech, *Forbes*, November 5, 2015, "https://www.forbes.com/sites/julianmitchell/2015/11/05/meet-morgan-debaun-the-blavity-founder-bridging-the-gap-between-content-and-tech/#23c94068751a. See also Bryan Logan, "How an LA Upstart is Redefining the Media World by Helping African-American Millennials 'Tell Their Own Story'," *Business Insider*, November 28, 2018, https://www.businessinsider.com/blavity-aaron-samuels-interview-business-insider-ignition-2018-2018-10.

[48] "Naa Hammond," *Groundswell Fund*, accessed November 7, 2017, https://groundswellfund.org/naa-hammond/.

[49] Abby Jones, "New Orleans for Houston- Benefit Concert w/ Big Freedia & More," *Universe*, accessed November 7, 2017, https://www.universe.com/events/new-orleans-for-houston-benefit-concert-w-big-freedia-more-tickets-D6503G. See also Lindsay Roberts, Amy Young, et. al, "20 Best Things to Do This Week in Metro Phoenix," *Phoenix New Times*, accessed November 7, 2017, www.phoenixnewtimes.com/arts/phoenix-best-events-august-2-august-9-big-freedia-war-on-the-catwalk-24-hour-theatre-project-9551404.

➤ Yara Shahidi's work with Saving Our Daughters (a nonprofit that creates opportunities for dialogue between teenage girls to discuss issues like bullying, dating abuse, domestic violence and more) and DoSomething.org (which encourages young women to enter STEM fields)[50]

➤ Beyoncé and JAY-Z who made donations to bail Black Lives Matter protesters out of jail[51]

➤ JAY-Z for his 4:44 album (particularly songs like "Legacy," "Story of O.J.," and "Smile") where he speaks of the value of investing, Black ownership, and generational wealth[52]

➤ Marshawn Lynch's work as cofounder of Fam 1st Family Foundation; Lynch is known for Fam 1st football camp for Bay area youth, buying soul food restaurant Scend's Restaurant and Bar, and giving away $58,000 worth in tickets to Oakland youth to go to Raging Waters[53]

---

[50] "Yara Shahidi Uses Her Star Power to Inspire and Create Change," *Points of Light*, accessed November 8, 2017, www.pointsoflight.org/blog/2016/06/29/yara-shahidi-uses-her-star-power-inspire-and-create-change.

[51] Michael Pearson, "Jay Z Posted Bail for Protesters, Writer Says," *CNN*, May 19, 2015, www.cnn.com/2015/05/19/entertainment/feat-jay-z-protesters-bail/index.html.

[52] Robby Seabrook III, "The Narrative of Jay-Z's '4:44' is Driven by the Value of Black Capitalism, *Genius*, July 1, 2017, https://genius.com/a/the-narrative-of-jay-z-s-4-44-is-driven-by-the-value-of-black-capitalism.

[53] "Fam1st Family Foundation," accessed November 10, 2017. https://fam1stfamilyfoundation.org/pages/about-us. See also Ellen Fort, "Marshawn Lynch Takes Over Emeryville Soul Food Restaurant to Save It," *Eater*, last modified July 19, 2017, https://sf.eater.com/2017/7/19/15998838/marshawn-lynch-scends-soul-food-emeryville-oakland. See also Sam Belden, "Marshawn Lynch Surprises Oakland Kids with 2,000 Free Water-Park Tickets," *Business Insider*, last modified June 29, 2017, www.businessinsider.com/marshawn-lynch-oakland-kids-free-waterpark-tickets-2017-6.

➤ Colin Kaepernick makes a pledge to donate $1,000,000 to organizations that work with marginalized communities which includes: $25,000 to Assata's Daughters, $25,000 to Causa Justa Just Cause, $25,000 to Black Youth Project, $25,000 to Communities United for Police Reform, $25,000 to DACA and other immigrant youth programs, and $50,000 to Mni Wiconi Health Clinic Partnership at Standing Rock[54]

➤ Filmmakers Ryan Coogler (*Creed, Fruitvale Station, Black Panther*) and Ava DuVernay (*Selma, 13th, A Wrinkle In Time*) and founding members of Blackout for Human Rights organized the benefit concert #JUSTICEFORFLINT hosted by Hannibal Buress featuring performances/appearances by Janelle Monáe, Ledisi, Andra Day, Musiq Soulchild, Jesse Williams, Jussie Smollet, Royce da 5'9", Vic Mensa, Stevie Wonder, and more[55]

➤ LeBron James opens the I PROMISE School[56]

➤ Oprah…where do I even begin?

[54] Marjua Estevez, "Colin Kaepernick Pledges $25,000 For Immigrant Youth and DACA Program," *Vibe*, last modified September 18, 2017, https://www.vibe.com/2017/09/colin-kaepernick-donates-25000-daca/?utm_source=twitter&utm_medium=social&utm_campaign=timeline. See also Jamilah King, "Colin Kaepernick Donated $25,000 to Black Women, and Conservatives Lost Their Minds," *Mother Jones*, last modified October 2, 2017, www.motherjones.com/crime-justice/2017/10/colin-kaepernick-donated-25000-to-black-women-and-conservatives-lost-their-minds/#. See also "Million Dollar Pledge," accessed November 10, 2017, http://kaepernick7.com.

[55] Sameer Rao, "Livestream: Watch #JUSTICEFORFLINT and Fight the Flint Water Crisis," *Colorlines*, February 26, 2016, https://www.colorlines.com/articles/livestream-watch-justiceforflint-and-fight-flint-water-crisis.

[56] "The LeBron James Family Foundation," accessed November 14, 2018. http://www.lebronjamesfamilyfoundation.org.

There are so many models in our community, past and present, who have shown us what it means to make wise, humanitarian choices with their wealth.

For us, the purpose of financial freedom and wealth-building is providing greater options for our children and our children's children. Options that are filled with rewarding, memorable experiences. Experiences that position them to make power moves that defy the structural forces that create systemic inequities. Instead of falling victim to the haphazard throes of perpetual struggle, our future generations will have the agency to shape their existence without interference...and be free to imagine, build, and give. Let these intentions be sealed by the divine Love of our Creator and the ancestors. *Ashe.*

Your Sister in Spirit,

Janet

LETTER #9: SELF-CARE (Part I)

June 5, 2018

To Black Parents Visiting Earth:

I hold stress in my body. Mostly in my back.

Sometimes I wake up three or four hours before my alarm goes off. My mind races. I'm problem-solving. I'm anxious. I'm worried. I'm building to-do lists in my head. I'm efficient. I'm effective. My body is well-trained as a loyal, hardworking American citizen—even at 3:00 am with my eyes closed.

There were many mornings when my mind was too loud and too fast. My chest tight. Placing my hand over my heart calmed me down when massaging my palms didn't work.

In March 2016, I called Kaiser Oakland and told them about the tightness in my chest. They told me to go to the ER, but I didn't think it was that serious.

Later that day, I called Kaiser Richmond and told them the same thing. They said, "Go to the ER." I said, "That's what I was told earlier, but I'm not so sure it's that bad." Then the nurse calmly said something like, "Well, if you were told this earlier, you do realize that if you choose not to go to the ER, you are refusing care?"

*

So, there I was, sitting in the ER, hooked up to an EKG machine, my husband and Baby Girl by my side. Cords from all over the place were attached to my body.

The nurses checked my heart. Checked my blood pressure. Took some X-rays. Drew some blood.

The results came in. Blood looked good. Blood pressure normal. No heart problems. Nothing wrong with any other organs. I was in stellar health.

"I'm happy everything's okay," I told the doctor, "but what can you attribute the chest pain to?"

He looked at me and said, "So, how's work?"

I burst into tears.

*

I used to enjoy work. I loved being in the classroom. Absolutely loved my students. But, outside the classroom, the volume of work became ridiculous and extremely poor administration made it impossible to be effective. I was miserable there, and it was spilling over into other areas of my life.

But it wasn't always this way.

In 2012, I wrote a self-care essay called, "A Perfect Ordinary Day." In the piece, I designed my own "perfect day" doing all the things I enjoy. I was ultimately sending the message that self-care is not selfish.[57] It is a necessary act of self-love—a love that reminds us of how important it is to feed ourselves with the "food" that nourishes the heart, mind, body, and spirit.

---

[57] Janet Stickmon, "A Perfect Ordinary Day," in *Midnight Peaches, Two O'clock Patience*, (Oakland: Broken Shackle Publishing, International, 2011), 133-154.

Back then, I was loving life; this made writing the essay easy. I was well-accomplished at work. I had the support and respect of many of my colleagues. I was growing stronger and more confident after three years of Muay Thai training. I was building muscle mass and loving the shape of my body. I had a solid group of friends who made me laugh and kept me motivated. Plenty of things were going well enough in my life to provide me with the energy that fueled my creativity and inspired me to sometimes even wake up at 1:00 or 2:00 a.m. to write.

Calling this unusual would be an understatement. I was light on me feet, fully alive, and glowing. My love for everything around me was overflowing. I was sparkly.[58] My writing felt divinely-inspired.[59] I rode that high for about two years until it gradually faded away.

Four years later, when fatigue became my greatest enemy—while time and punk-ass people were a close second—I decided to read that essay; I thought I just needed to follow my own advice to get out of the rut I was in. But reading it didn't make me feel any better. I found myself focusing less on the message of feeding myself emotionally, spiritually, and physically and more on why I wasn't as clear and vibrant as I used to be. That article was written during a moment of clarity and confidence; but when I reread it four years later, I was anything but clear and confident. I was off-balance. I was full of self-doubt. I was constantly worried about everything. Always angry and bitter.

The more I read that piece, the more frustrated I became. I was deeply disappointed in myself. *How could I be so clear before, but now be so confused?*

---

[58] A former student of mine, Edgar-Arturo Camacho Gonzalez (cofounder of El Comalito Collective) introduced this word into my vocabulary one day when he called me sparkly at a time when I didn't feel very sparkly. It has since remained a part of my daily consciousness—an ideal that I aspire to embody half as well as he does.

[59] That self-care essay found its way into my book *Midnight Peaches, Two O'clock Patience* which took only about a year and half to write—record time for me.

The activities of that perfect ordinary day (and the beliefs that supported them) were real and true for me at the time I wrote the essay, but they just didn't fit anymore. My surroundings looked different to me; they didn't have meaning. I was bored with my routine. I was four years older and had outgrown what was once so familiar.

My life needed to be different somehow; it needed to be lighter, fuller. I wanted my sparkle back. I wasn't exactly sure what this was supposed to look like, but it had to happen soon. What fed me before no longer brought me the same joy. With age, my likes, dislikes, and tolerances changed, and so my self-care needs had to change too.

*

Shortly after the ER visit, I had a nice phone conversation with Dr. Singh, my doctor. His voice was sincere and his words had a gentle, even pace. The whole feel of those first few seconds made me think he might have something new to tell me.

As expected, he spoke about the importance of diet and exercise. He recommended a therapist. Then about halfway in, he spoke about the impact of work-related stress. After a certain point, I forgot his exact words and only remembered feeling a bit transparent but also at peace. I think he was all too familiar with people like me.

"So, what do you do for fun?" Dr. Singh asked. Such a simple question felt like a set-up. But, I answered it. Not very well if memory serves me correctly. My answer must not have been too impressive because by the time I was done, he ultimately had to prescribe fun.

Fun? This seemed almost groundbreaking to hear from a physician. It was a pleasant surprise, but also confusing. I thought I was a fun person. *Why would a fun person need advice like this?* Then it occurred to me that my fun self must not be having so much fun if my ass wound up in the ER!

*

I've always pushed myself to be as disciplined as possible, putting efficiency and productivity first, foregoing gratification until all (or most) of the work was done. Call it the overachiever, perfectionist, scholar-athlete in me or the value for excellence my mom instilled in me. Call it the orphan in me, afraid of ending up on the streets. Call it the woman of color in me, always prepared for unwarranted scrutiny.

As a child and teenager, I always concentrated on getting better, measuring my success by: 1) how much I improved, 2) how many trophies or plaques I won, 3) how many A's I earned, or 4) how much praise the teacher gave me. The objective was to work hard enough to be the best, get noticed, and play later. As an adult, the objective remained the same. This mentality—one I'd grown quite proud of—served me well for most of my life. But when you take it too far, you pay a price.

I lost many nights of sleep because of work. Despite my exhaustion, I continued to plow through never-ending to-do lists, always stressed about not having enough time to finish everything. I'd beat myself up over inconsequential flaws, focused on the one thing that went wrong as opposed to everything else that went right. Not only was this unhealthy, but I showed no compassion toward myself. I would never be cruel enough to push anyone else beyond the point of exhaustion, beat them up for all the mistakes they made, force them to wait until all the work was perfect before I would finally say, "Ok, now you can eat. Now you can sleep. Now you can go have fun." If I would never do this to other people, why would I do this to myself?

I see friends and acquaintances doing similar unkind things to themselves. Some end up far worse off than me. Young and old, they lose sleep, don't eat, don't exercise, don't celebrate, and will still try to work hard and fight hard. I've watched them get sick. I've watched colds, flus, hives, high blood pressure, heart attacks, anxiety attacks, heart disease, strokes, cancer, gastro-intestinal problems, insomnia, pneumonia, and depression bring them to their knees, finally making them question their invincibility. For some, neglecting one's basic needs seemed like a small sacrifice if it meant they were transforming lives and outrunning evil. But then their bodies collapsed.

Some claim they can't rest because there's more work to be done, more progress to be made; some believe that if they stop, they might get soft or get spoiled. They want to stay ready, stay engaged in the struggle to dismantle the evil that causes injustice…because evil never sleeps.

Okay, well, evil won't pay your medical bills either!

I've seen one too many peers and elders literally work themselves to death, never having the chance to enjoy life. I've seen people unravel emotionally, suffer from chronic illnesses, or die before they have the chance to retire.

I want something different for myself.

I'm keeping my value for personal excellence, never letting it blind me to the excellence of others. I'm keeping my compassion, vigilance, and righteous anger, remembering to be kind enough to myself to always prioritize rest. I'm keeping my 2012 perfect ordinary day, but will integrate a bit of that perfect day into every day. I'm keeping the precision of that overachiever, but will be at peace with my mistakes and ambivalence, knowing they will always give birth to creativity. I will reclaim my playful side and regain my sparkle. I will live a long, joyful life. *Ashe.*

Rejuvenating myself can no longer be one of those things I do after all the work is done or whenever I have extra time. Self-care must to be integrated into my daily routine like vitamins. Ultimately, I must view my self-care regimen as essential and not a luxury.

Self-care needs to be fun, healthy, loving ways of thanking myself for all that I am and all that I do.[60] Considering how much heart I put into everything I

---

[60] With this, I can hear Glenn Noronha, an old friend of mine from my undergraduate years at U.C. Irvine, telling me, "Be kind to yourself."

do in life, the least I could do is show my body, mind, and spirit a little gratitude and compassion…showing myself that I am worthy of my own love.

There are certain basics like working out and eating right that just aren't optional anymore. In my twenties, I could get away with not stretching and exercising or not eating fruit and vegetables and still remain fairly healthy.[61] But now in my forties, the absence of healthy habits makes itself known through aches and pains, crappy sleep, low energy, a foul mood, and poor judgment. Taking care of myself must become a priority if I say I love myself.

Today I declare that: stretching is no longer optional. Exercise is not optional. Moisturizing is not optional. Drinking water is not optional. Watching my Vitamin C, calcium, iron, and magnesium intake is not optional. Taking daily vitamins is no longer optional. Eating fruit and vegetables is not optional. Sleeping well is not optional. Playing, wandering, vacationing, and taking regular breaks are no longer optional. Being in the presence of good, sparkly people is not optional. If I want to begin to live a life filled with joy, I must consciously integrate all these things into my daily life to serve as a foundation I can build on.

As I build this foundation, let me remember to not be so rigid. May I continue to be disciplined, but also allow for greater fluidity, flexibility, and flow. *Ashe.*

Love always,

Janet

---

[61] In retrospect, if I made better choices regarding diet and exercise during my undergraduate years, I'm sure I would have been a lot less sluggish.

LETTER #10: SELF-CARE (Part II)

July 8, 2018

To Black Parents Visiting Earth,

Self-care and being Black. The topic is a little more complicated than just saying, "Go exercise. Relax. Take a break." The simple things that constitute rest and relaxation for most folks signal potential danger if you're Black.

For example, you know how doctors might recommend walking 30 minutes/day? I know my husband doesn't always have the flexibility to squeeze this in during the day, so he waits until he gets off work. Sometimes, he doesn't get home until dark. As a Black man, he doesn't feel safe walking alone in our neighborhood—day or night. And when we consider he's been harassed by the cops in our own driveway, this is one more reason to stay indoors and take a walk some other time.

Whether we're worried about the cops or worried about the BBQ Beckies of the world calling the cops on us for barbecuing, sitting down at Starbucks, or falling asleep in the common room of our own dorm, our bodies become cause for suspicion in spaces where white bodies feel threatened, where white people believe they are the only ones entitled to and deserving of occupying such spaces. The ultimate message: "You're a nuisance. You're dangerous. You don't belong here!" Hmm. Sounds an awful lot like what fueled post-Civil War vagrancy laws.

We can't let any of this keep us in the house all day, but we can't ignore the fact that this garbage—all the stuff that makes us fear for our safety and our overall well-being—interferes with our ability to take care of ourselves. How do we care for ourselves amidst the anti-Blackness?

*

One of the realities of Black life in the U.S. is how often it gets interrupted by wholesale tragedy (as you've seen in my previous letters). Knowing this, I'm still not so quick to say that being Black is strictly defined by tragedy and the struggles that come with that tragedy. We can't ignore or run from our individual or collective tragedies, that's for sure; the scars they leave behind cannot be denied. However, allowing tragedy to be our distinguishing characteristic as a people can be dangerous and unhealthy. It allows us and others to jump too quickly to the conclusion that we are, and always will be, a damaged, fragile, helpless people. It flirts too much with things akin to deficit models in education or scarcity/deprivation mentalities, the latter being all too common among some who confuse the struggle with their identity or believe that communities of color are destined to live lives of perpetual struggle, considering it even virtuous.

I believe what defines us as a people is our resiliency: the strength and beauty that develops within the soul as we work through and beyond tragedies we never chose. We cannot credit tragedy for this wonder. There is a power within that is much older. For something to bounce back, for something to resist, for something to bloom, there must be some fundamental power that precedes the tragedy, making it possible to withstand the tragedy in the first place. This makes me think of the power at the core of humanity coming from the Creator and how Zulu philosophers used the phrase *Umuntu Ngumuntu* meaning "the person is human." Through this concept, they taught that "the human person was unique in that the person defined oneself and is essentially knowledgeable of one's own intrinsic value."[62] Herein lies the

---

[62] In the *Izaga*, an ancient text that contains the Zulu interpretations of the teachings of the Sudic philosophy, the Zulu use the phrase, *Umuntu Ngumuntu*. See Wade Nobles, "To Be African or Not to Be: The Question of Identity or Authenticity—Some Preliminary Thoughts," in *Seeking the Sakhu: Foundational Writings for an African Psychology*, (Chicago: Third World Press, 2006), 333.

secret to our capacity for resiliency. As long as we remember that we possess the fundamental power to actively define ourselves and know how valuable we are, we can push right through anything that tries to strip us of our humanity.

Now, of course this doesn't mean we don't bruise and bleed. This doesn't mean we should become the play thing of those with contempt for the Black body and be subjected to all kinds of violence because they think we can "handle it"; this doesn't mean that we should be verbally abused by those who justify their actions by claiming they are teaching "grit."

An important caveat here is that resiliency has the potential to expand and grow as long as there is space and time to heal...*and* as long as we have several wins, several triumphs along the way. If not, we won't bounce back and get stronger. We'll just get brittle and break.

If we consider that resiliency is what defines us as a people, we can be in the frame of mind to think about the cultural and social capital we possess. What does this capital—our assets—look like? How does this country benefit from and rely on the assets existing prior to and those born daily against a backdrop of tragedy? How can this capital be used to directly serve and benefit our own communities?

If we seek to take care of our emotional and spiritual well-being as Black people, then part of that task begins with changing our language and interrupting the thoughts that tempt us into believing that tragedy and death is all that awaits us. Granted, doing this when our lives are constantly under attack seems virtually impossible, but we must carve out moments of respite, spaces of refuge. We have to. Our sanity, our survival, our prosperity depends on it.

We must prepare our minds to be ready to recognize, accept, and create abundance. Dr. Mario Martinez, a clinical neuropsychologist who developed the theory of biocognition, defines abundance as "...the amount of health, wealth, and love that you require in order to lead a joyful life...a wellness life…"[63] When abundance arrives, we need to be in a position to welcome it and embrace it.

If one has lived a life of deprivation (i.e. gone without food, love, safety, or financial stability, struggle to have one's dignity affirmed, rendered invisible and devalued by systems of oppression, experienced multiple deaths of loved ones, and/or any combination of these), there is a way in which the body and mind grow accustomed to this. Martinez argues that deprivation can be internalized by the immune, nervous, and endocrine system. In such a case, when abundance or joy enters our lives, our body then develops a stress response to it because it's foreign; we can become sick or engage in self-sabotage, ultimately rejecting the abundance we claimed to seek.[64] Using Martinez's meditation and visualization exercises gives you the chance to practice raising what he calls the "ceilings of abundance." By picturing abundance, paying attention to how certain parts of the body respond, and then breathing into those parts of the body where we may experience tension, we can be on the path toward slowly integrating that abundance into our system.[65]

Integrating abundance into our lives will require a change in the cognitive frames that have limited and distorted our ways of thinking about our own worthiness, self-care, influence on others, and proclivity for success. It can strengthen our emotional and spiritual well-being. This shift in consciousness can be achieved through the guidance of mental health professionals, indigenous healers, support groups, spiritual/religious communities, and a group of friends and family who know us well and love us well; it can also include a combination of practices, such as meditation, prayer, affirmations, mental rehearsal or visualization, and gratitude exercises. A mental and

---

[63] Mario Martinez, *The Mind-Body Code: How the Mind Wounds and Heals the Body*, Success, (Boulder: Sounds True, 2009), 6 compact discs; 7 hrs.

[64] Ibid.

[65] Ibid. You will find this particular exercise on Track 8 of the first CD. Typically, his meditation/visualization exercises are on the "Experiential Tools" track at the end of each CD. However, I strongly recommend listening to the entire CD to give you context and background prior to diving into the exercises.

spiritual wellness regimen consisting of the above will not only help us recognize and fully enjoy abundance when it comes but also allow us to hold onto it long enough to break the cycle of transgenerational trauma so abundance (not pain) is what we pass onto future generations.[66]

*

Abundance has been a recurring theme in my life for the past five years. Around 2013, it began with Mario Martinez's definition of abundance— again, the amount of health, wealth, and love needed to have a joyful life. Since then, I have embraced this definition of abundance as my own and have gradually learned to recognize, welcome, and invite abundance into my life.[67] Three years later, thanks to energy worker and intuitive guide, Hasnaa At-Tauhidi (Maryam Hasnaa), who teaches mysticism and metaphysics, I began understanding abundance as the rule and not the exception; that as human beings, God intends for us to enjoy abundance all the time, not just every now and then. As I get accustomed to this new idea, I seek to remember that I deserve to feel a sense of abundance everyday and that it's unnecessary to question its presence or worry about how long it will last.

So, in the spirit of abundance, I share with you a list of ways I integrate regular doses of joy and self-gratitude into my life. It reflects the sights and sounds, fragrances and textures that allow me to feel good. It includes activities and creature comforts that make me happy. Through this, I am reminded that I deserve to enjoy abundance on a regular basis.

Below you will find that I've divided the list into "daily practices" (i.e. things to do everyday), "weekly practices" (i.e. things to do every week), and

---

[66] This section was adapted from an excerpt of my essay "Honest and Good: A Reflection on *Invisible Man, Got the Whole World Watching*" in January 2017. See Janet Stickmon, "Honest and Good: A Reflection on *Invisible Man, Got the Whole World Watching*," *Books are Not a Luxury*, https://booksarenotaluxury.com/tag/invisible-man-got-the-whole-world-watching/.

[67] Since Mario Martinez, the neuroscience work of Srini Pillay, Mark Waldman, Rick Hanson, and John Assaraf have also had an impact on my path toward wellness.

"ongoing practices" (i.e. things I plan to integrate into my life more regularly throughout each month, throughout each year). Following some of the items, I included brief reflections to remind myself why the activity feeds my spirit.

My goal is to be 85-95% successful at integrating these practices into my life. So far, so good. When I don't reach my goal, I don't beat myself up about the things I miss; I affirm myself for what I have done and remind myself that there's always tomorrow.[68]

I hope these lists can serve as a model of how you can create your own set of self-care practices that suit your personal needs and passions. Please don't feel bound by anything here. If you want, feel free to use, rework, or augment anything you see below. Whatever self-care plan you design for yourself, don't forget to have fun!

Daily Practices
> Sleep (8 hours)

> Begin the day reflecting on William's (Ron Cephas Jones) advice to his son Randall (Sterling K. Brown) in *This is Us*: "Roll all your windows down, Randall. Crank up the music, grow out that fro, let someone else make your bed…You deserve the beautiful life you've made."

> Meditate (15-20 min. twice/day)
Reflection: For many years, I could sit in silent meditation for about 15 minutes without a mantra. I simply closed my eyes, took three deep breaths, and let go of all thought and made myself present to God. If there were any distractions, I lifted them up to God and recentered myself. Then for some reason I stopped, and when I tried to return to this practice, it didn't work out so well. A student recommended the Headspace app to me a few years ago. For a month, I used it religiously. Every so often, I bounced between Headspace and listening to the

---

[68] One thing I've noticed is that as I develop healthy habits, I get to the point where I genuinely miss the activity if I skip a day.

music of Chris Beaty or Otto Wahl while repeating a mantra. Lately, I've been using the guided meditations on Mario Martinez's Mind-Body Code CDs and Michael Bernard Beckwith's Life Visioning CDs. I'm not always successful at meditating everyday, but I look forward to doing it more often. It calms me down. It centers me.

➤ Green smoothie every morning:
  o   1/4 lb. baby spring mix
  o   5 oz açai juice
  o   5 oz coconut water
  o   Optional: chia seeds, turmeric, honey, kefir or plain yogurt

➤ Drink 3-4 bottles of water a day

➤ Take daily vitamins
  o   vegan multivitamin
  o   omega-3's

➤ Eat fruit and vegetables
  Reflection: I need to bring beets and avocadoes back into my life. I can eat 'em, but they're not my favorites. Just need to find more creative ways of preparing them.[69]

➤ Swimming (30 minutes, 3-5 days/week)
  Reflection: I once swam for speed and endurance. Now I practice form and flow. No longer do I focus on counting my laps. Instead, I practice play and surrender...sometimes mixing up the strokes, switching directions, and spontaneously twirling in circles like some kind of synchronized swimmer. When I swim, I feel refreshed and energized. I like the way the pool smells. All the lifeguards know me. No one (actually, just one person) knows what I do for a living...which is nice because sometimes I like being in spaces that remind me

---

[69] Some of these dietary habits may change since I recently completed a 30-day detox through www.thedetoxnow.com. Looking forward to seeing what those changes look like.

that my profession is not my identity. No one evaluates my performance. It is inspiring to be surrounded by people 20-30 years older than me who also prioritize their health. Life is good in the water.

➢ Soft gaze at my vision board

➢ Listen to or write down affirmations

➢ Before bedtime, write down five things from that day that I am grateful for.

➢ Pray

Weekly Practices

➢ Painting class (once a week)
Reflection: I go because I want to learn. Painting calms me down. There's no deadline to demonstrate improvement. The teacher is kind and youthful. She welcomes my daughter and sometimes they dance together on the patio. My classmates know little to nothing about what I do for a living. In fact, our professions (or former professions for the retirees in the class) rarely enter the conversation. My classmates are very warm and caring people. We break bread together.

➢ Bikram Yoga (at least twice/week)
Reflection: It is the one space where I can move and pray at the same time. The owner of the studio is Black. I usually attend his sessions because he has a melodic voice that helps me feel happy and encouraged. The class is ethnically diverse. I remember looking across the front row one day, and 7 out of the 9 of us were people of color...four of us Black. I have the opportunity to practice looking myself in the eye and looking at my body and liking what I see.

➢ Go to the Parkour gym (at least once a week)

➢ Meditate on my Wu-Tang name: Sarkastik Overlord

- Write (16-25 hours a week)

- Read

- Soak in the hot tub

- Listen to French horn music

- Day-long dates with my husband

- Spend time with friends and relatives

- Kayaking

- Eat crunchy food
  Reflection: I am addicted to potato chips. I am a chip fiend. I thought it was maybe the crunch that I was addicted to so I tried eating everything from nuts, sunflower seeds, and snap pea crisps to sweet potato chips, beet chips, blue corn chips, and plantain chips instead. Sigh. It just wasn't the same. After a year of trying to kick this habit, my husband came home one day with a bag of yucca chips. Ah, yes, I think I'll be just fine.

- Sit at a coffeeshop

- Go to the beach and walk along the shore

- Keep the following nearby at all times: eye pillow, Parker pens, Carmex, small journal

- Watch *Happily Ever After: Fairy Tales for Every Child*, *Adventure Time*, *Steven Universe*, and *We Bare Bears* with Baby Girl

- Watch *Rasta Mouse*, *Hunter Street*, *Deep*, *Butter and Brown*, and *Great British Baking Show* with my family

➢ Watch *Martin* especially the following clips:
  o Myra's feet ("Control," Season 2, Episode 7)
  o Rent 'Em Spoons!! ("C.R.E.A.M.," Season 3, Episode 22)
  o Almond Brown ("DMV Blues," Season 4, Episode 25)

➢ Watch any episode of *In Living Color* that includes sketches of:
  o Snackin' Shack
  o Wanda
  o Calhoun Tubbs

Ongoing Practices
➢ Foot massage

➢ Full body massage

➢ Pedicure

➢ Facial

➢ Buy flowers

➢ Set boundaries: Practice saying no to tasks that aren't aligned with my personal goals

➢ Get a Raspberry Dazzle cupcake from Kara's Cupcakes

➢ Walk in puddles

➢ Watch clip of Uncle Pecos singing "Crambone" (from *Tom and Jerry*)

➢ Watch *Living Single*: any episode

➢ Watch Zendaya lip sync "24K Magic" on *Lip Sync Battle*

➢ Listen to Oprah's podcasts: *SuperSoul Conversations* and *Master Class*

➤ Watch *Red Table Talk* with Jada Pinkett-Smith

➤ Watch *Last Holiday, Dave Chappelle's Block Party,* and *Katt Williams' It's Pimpin' Pimpin'*

➤ Read Black Twitter tweets like:
   ○ #BBQBecky memes
   ○ #OaklandCookout
   ○ "You Got the Wrong One, Bitch" by Amanda Seales (music by Brian Alexander Morgan)

➤ Play Hair Nah (Hairnah.com)

➤ Refrain from organizing or uttering the words "work retreat" or "working lunch"
   Reflection: These are oxymorons. Either work or eat lunch. Go on retreat or go to work. You can't do both. I find conflating the two is a scary way work bleeds into our breaks and leisure time. It's just one more way the warped U.S. work ethic subtly drains the life from working people. And it's just not healthy for your system.

➤ Read aloud in the livingroom with the family

➤ Go on picnics

➤ Listen to my favorite songs. Here are the latest:

The Beloved Diaspora Mix

"Exu- Nation Ketou (Awo)," Traditionnel
"Oshun Chant," Women of the Calabash
"Kemekem (I Like Your Afro)," Meklit
"La Verdolaga," Totó la Momposina
"La Negra Tiene Tumbao," Celia Cruz

"Lift Every Voice and Sing," The Wardlaw Brothers
"We Built This," Cast of Black-ish
"Okra," Olu Dara
"Roots Woman," Corey Harris
"Feeling Good," Nina Simone
"Ain't Got No – I Got Life," Nina Simone
"Take Me To The Alley," Gregory Porter
"I Think I'll Call It Morning," Gil Scott-Heron
"When You Are Who You Are," Gil Scott-Heron
"Outstanding," The Gap Band
"Glory," Common and John Legend
"Black America Again," Common, Stevie Wonder
The Revolution Will Not Be Televised, Gil Scott-Heron
"The Story of O.J.," JAY-Z
"Freedom," Beyoncé, (feat. Kendrick Lamar)
"Formation," Beyoncé
"When Doves Cry," Prince
"Confrontation," Damian Marley and Nas
"Fu-Gee-La," Fugees
"The System," Popcaan
"Notorious (Vital Elements Remix)," Nãnci & Phoebe
"Bring The Noise," Public Enemy
"Fix Up, Look Sharp," Dizzee Rascal
"21 Seconds," So Solid Crew
"Apeshit," The Carters
"Here We Go Again," Roots Manuva
"Neva Soft (RMX)," Ms. Dynamite x Amplify Dot x Lady Lashurr x Lioness
"Lagos Town," Afrikan Boy
"Wavin' Flag," K'naan

Claimin' Space Mix

"O.G.," TroyBoi
"Uknowhowwedu," Bahamadia
"I Dare You," Black Rob, (feat. Joe Hooker)

"Stronger Than You," Estelle
"This is Me," Keala Settle
"Legend Has It," Run the Jewels
"Baby Baby," Tropkillaz
"KinjaBang," TroyBoi
"One Here Comes the Two," Tropkillaz
"Black Panther," Lady Leshurr
"Destinations," Gesaffelstein
"Skwod," Nadia Rose
"Skelewu," DaVido
"This Is America," Childish Gambino
"This Is Nigeria," Falz
"Pray For Me," The Weeknd, Kendrick Lamar
"Sincerely, Jane," Janelle Monáe
"Cranes in the Sky," Solange
"Don't Touch My Hair" Solange, (feat. Sampha)
"Best of Me," Anthony Hamilton
"All I Do Is Think of You," Troop
"Candy Rain," Soul for Real
"Every Little Thing I Do," Soul for Real
"24K Magic," Bruno Mars
"After Party," Koffee Brown
"Massage Situation," Flying Lotus
"Sweet Dreams," Beyoncé
"Explode," Big Freedia
"Automatic," ZHU x AlunaGeorge
"Dove," Pillar Point
"Save the World/Don't Worry Child," Pentatonix
"Stay, Runaway," The Bullitts (feat. Doxi Jones)
"RedBone," Childish Gambino
"Back Pocket," Vulfpeck
"Attention (Remix)," Charlie Puth, (feat. Kyle)
"Sorry," Beyoncé
"Tender Love," TroyBoi
"All The Stars," Kendrick Lamar (feat. SZA)

"Kármán Line," Copperwire (Meklit's lyrics)

When you finish reading this letter, please sit down and design your own self-care regimen. Give yourself the freedom to adjust it as your likes and dislikes change. My ultimate personal goal is that as I practice taking good care of myself, I will serve as a good model for my daughter. If she sees me taking care of myself, then she will learn the value of taking care of herself.

Wishing you well,

Janet

LETTER #11: EDUCATION

July 11, 2018

To Black Parents Visiting Earth:

On Halloween morning, an incident took place between my daughter and one of her 4th grade teachers. When she told me about it, I asked her to write it down. Here's what she wrote:

> Today at school when I asked Ms. Jones where the band-aids were she said "Really? After yesterday you still don't know where they are?" Then I said "I don't think you should be talking to me in that tone." Then, Ms. Jones said "Well I'm sorry, but I just dealt with a conflict so I have alot on my plate right now." Then I said "Just because you had a conflict at recess doesn't mean you have to be rude to me." Then Ms. Jones said in a whiny voice, "It's not my fault that you don't know where the band-aids are. It's your fault. You were wrong." Then I went back to my seat and just cried. When I was at my seat Leslie, Karen, and Lita asked if I was ok.[70]

Since the beginning of the school year, Baby Girl documented 13 incidents of teacher misconduct—evidence of teachers exhibiting behaviors that were, at best, not conducive to a positive learning environment. Some of these were directed at her, some directed at other students, and some toward the entire class. The day before Halloween, my husband had a meeting with the principal to talk about these incidents. This wasn't the first of such exchanges.

---

[70] Names were changed. Spelling and punctuation left unedited.

Since the meeting just took place, we were beyond frustrated to hear that a day later, the band-aid incident happened. Did the principal reprimand the teacher(s) for their past behavior? Did he at least talk to them? If so, did they care? Was Ms. Jones retaliating against my child?

We may never know. At the time, it almost didn't matter because within an hour after Baby Girl told me what happened, I received news that this would be the last day anyone at that school could hurt my child.

*

Baby Girl's new school was a closed campus. The only entrance was through the administration office. As we walked in that first day, Ms. Nikki and Ms. Lorelai said hi with big smiles and welcomed Baby Girl in by name. To my left was a sign that read: "Love Your Neighbor…Your Black, Brown, White, Native American, Immigrant, Disabled, Religiously Different, LGBTQ, Fully Human Neighbor."

Ms. Lorelai consulted with Ms. Nikki as she gathered the forms I needed to fill out. Ms. Lorelai asked me, "Is she GATE-identified?" I said no, but my no was a little clumsy; the question caught me off guard. How nice it was to be asked a question framed in a way that assumed my child was intelligent.

"Ok, we'll just make sure she's tested the next time around…and we already know who your teacher's going to be. Her name is Ms. Ernvark, and she'll have your space ready for you on Monday." Baby Girl nodded and smiled. I sat down to fill out the paperwork. Ms. Lorelai and Ms. Nikki were up and down from their desks, doing triage, tending to every concern as the phone rang and parents walked in the door. They had a swift, fun grace about them, their friendly banter interrupted by laughs here and there.

"My apologies. I know I'm taking a long time with this paperwork," I told them. "I just want to make sure I have all the details right."

"Oh, don't worry. You're fine. Make yourself right at home," Ms. Lorelai said. "We're like a family here." I've heard this before. I wasn't sure if I could trust these words or not, but I wanted to.

"I wish I could tell you how happy I am to hear that. I really wish I could."

A part of me was hoping they could read between the lines. I was holding back a lot. It was a strange thing having gratitude choked between wanting to be expressed and not wanting to sound pathetic. I wasn't sure how much they already knew about my daughter's situation. Something told me they may at least have an idea, partly because of my meeting with the principal the week before and partly because of the timing of it all: parents wouldn't pull their child out of school in the middle of a semester—and have her go to a school in a different district, in a different county—if the circumstances weren't serious.

*

This school had high ratings. We heard good things about it from relatives. We figured perhaps this school would be a place where she could rest from battle…be in a new place where her intelligence could be nurtured and leadership skills recognized. Overall, we wanted her to be able to learn and have a positive experience.

For a couple months, things seemed good. The school was winning points with us. I even believed the school could be a good model for how others could create foundational structures that support learning. Baby Girl was cautious, but slowly opening up and learning to trust her new environment.

Time goes on, and then I realize something is off. I remember there were a few red flags early on, but I dismissed them because I didn't want to zero in on flaws that might not be a big deal. I also ignored these issues because I felt like we had limited options and this seemed to be the best one for the time being. When your child goes so long without a strong, affirming education, you tend to see all the good things in the new environment. Everything seemed so fresh and new and cutting edge. Even the school bell was pleasant; Baby Girl said it sounded like a cow singing opera.

Long story short, the new school was an improvement over the last, particularly when it came to the kindness of the office staff, the quality of some of class assignments, the skill of some of the instructors, the familiarity with online learning tools, and the ongoing email communication with parents. However, not everything improved. Some things were the same. And some were worse. It wasn't exactly what I was expecting.

For the record, I wasn't expecting perfection. Never was. At the very least, in the 21st century in California, I was expecting that K-12 teachers would have a basic understanding about their own unconscious bias and the importance of integrating the narratives of various ethnic groups into the curriculum. In retrospect, I had no concrete reason for believing this. Perhaps what gave me an ounce of hope was that "Love Your Neighbor" sign in the front office. However, I knew the sign was no evidence of deep cultural competence or cultural humility, but it still gave me a bit of hope.

I suppose that after everything she'd been through, I was hoping Baby Girl could escape further scarring from institutionalized whiteness: the type that most white people don't realize exists; the type that some people of color buy into and refuse to see; the type that nice white people would say is a thing of the past; the kind that reduces our experiences to a perception of reality while that of white people remains the reality; the type white teachers don't speak of because they want so badly to be viewed as "one of those cool white people" lest their students of color turn against them; the type that sees no need in incorporating the perspectives of various ethnic groups into the curriculum for fear that doing so would become divisive; the kind that wants to be seen as "just" human, objective, and neutral.

George Lipsitz describes it by saying, "Whiteness is everywhere in U.S. culture, but it is very hard to see."[71]

Richard Dyer says, "Whites must be seen to be white, yet whiteness as race resides in invisible properties and whiteness as power is maintained by being unseen."[72] Dyer states, "…because we are seen as white, we characteristically

---

[71] George Lipsitz, *The Possessive Investment in Whiteness: How White People Profit From Identity Politics* (Philadelphia: Temple University Press, 1998), 1.
[72] Richard Dyer, *White* (New York: Routledge, 1997), 45.

see ourselves and believe ourselves seen as unmarked, unspecific, universal."[73] Whiteness is the default and as such, it thrives from slipping past our attention.

As prevalent as institutionalized whiteness is in our schools, we must examine how culturally relevant teaching—a term coined by Gloria Ladson-Billings in the 1990s—would mitigate its harmful effects. Ladson-Billings explains:

> Thus culturally relevant teaching uses student culture in order to maintain it and to transcend the negative effects of the dominant culture. The negative effects are brought about, for example, by not seeing one's history, culture, or background represented in the textbook or curriculum or by seeing that history, culture, or background distorted. Or they may result from the staffing pattern in the school (when all teachers and the principal are white and only the janitors and cafeteria workers are African American, for example) and from the tracking of African American students into the lowest-level classes.[74]

The power of institutionalized whiteness was what I hoped my child could escape from or perhaps be unscathed by. Yet, I had no evidence that the teachers in that district had undergone any training in culturally relevant or culturally responsive teaching. No training in Ethnic Studies.[75] No evidence that they received training about cultural competence and cultural humility.[76]

---

[73] Ibid.

[74] Gloria Ladson-Billings, *The Dreamkeepers: Successful Teachers of African American Children* (San Francisco: John Wiley & Sons, Inc., 2009), 19-20.

[75] Christine Sleeter, "The Academic and Social Value of Ethnic Studies," *National Education Association*, accessed July 11, 2018, http://www.nea.org/assets/docs/NBI-2010-3-value-of-ethnic-studies.pdf. See also Allyson Tintiangco-Cubales, et. al, "Toward an Ethnic Studies Pedagogy: Implications for K-12 Schools from Research," *The Urban Review: Issues and Ideas in Public Education* 47, no. 1(2015), accessed July 11, 2018, https://www.academia.edu/6545474/Toward_an_Ethnic_Studies_Pedagogy_Implications_for_K-12_Schools_from_the_Research.

[76] Melanie Tervalon and Jann Murray-Garcia, "Cultural Humility Versus Cultural Competence: A Critical Distinction in Defining Physician Training Outcomes in Multicultural Education," *Journal of Healthcare for the Poor and Underserved* 9, no. 2(1998): 117-125, http://melanietervalon.com/wp-

No evidence that they had done any work recognizing their own unconscious biases and the microaggressions stemming from these biases that affect students and their families. No evidence that they understood the impact of systems of oppression and privilege. No evidence that they understood the difference between deficit and equity cognitive frames or evidence that equity-mindedness was built into their institution.[77] No evidence that they ensured that the perspectives of, the narratives of different underrepresented ethnic groups (especially those that made up their student population) were integrated across the curriculum.

As a parent, IF you ask whether or not teachers, staff, and administrators have training in the areas above, and: 1) there is no unequivocal "yes" coming from administration, office staff, and teachers, along with examples of how this training is put into practice, 2) a value for such pedagogy isn't reflected in the mission or vision statement or in the core values/beliefs/goals of the institution and the district, 3) there are no documents on the school and district website demonstrating that district-organized, district-wide professional development in all of the above is taking place, and 4) you don't hear parents and students of color talking about seeing their cultural histories and experiences reflected in the curriculum, THEN it's only a matter of time before the lack of training in these areas becomes painfully obvious to you and your child.

*

content/uploads/2013/08/CulturalHumility_Tervalon-and-Murray-Garcia-Article.pdf.

[77] "What is Equity-Mindedness?" *University of Southern California, Center for Urban Education*, accessed July 11, 2018, https://cue.usc.edu/equity/equity-mindedness/; Estela Bensimon gives a succinct comparison of deficit and equity cognitive frames. See also Estela Bensimon, "Learning Equity-Mindedness: Equality in Educational Outcomes," *New England Resource Center for Higher Education-The Academic Workplace* 17, no. 1 (2006): 4-5, https://cue.usc.edu/files/2016/01/Bensimon_Learning-Equity-Mindedness-Equality-in-Educational-Outcomes.pdf.

Between the ages of 7 and 10, at the hands of educators, Baby Girl has experienced numerous incidents that were either disrespectful, childish, dismissive, disempowering, racist, sexist, homophobic, or a combination thereof. Among these educators were teachers (including substitutes) and administrators at school, tutors and teaching assistants in afterschool or extracurricular programs, summer camp instructors, and coaches. In each of these spaces, the majority of them were white educators serving predominantly students of color.[78] These incidents included educators: responding with anger or sarcasm when she or other students asked clarifying questions (assuming in my daughter's case that her question meant she was not paying attention); banging on tables and yelling to get students to listen; physically moving her and other students in a hurtful, uncomfortable and/or inappropriate way; writing cryptic messages on the board to scare students into listening; equating the students to animals (i.e. monkeys and dogs); making inappropriate comments about her hair (and touching her hair); making sexist comments regarding physical ability; dismissing sexist statements made by teachers; drawing unnecessary attention to her by accusing her of being a distraction to the class when she was helping another student; responding with anger when she or other students gave the wrong answer to a question; confusing her with the only other Black student in class; engaging in victim-blaming and gaslighting; telling her that instruction about LGBTQ experiences won't happen for fear that some parents will object; giving the class an assignment to write about the Dred Scott case from the perspective of the slaveowner; wrongfully accusing her of being disruptive or of rolling her eyes; making disrespectful, flippant remarks that either intentionally or inadvertently shame students into changing their behavior; telling her that the #MeToo movement was inappropriate for school; telling the whole class "You are going to fail"; not believing her (and other students) when she was telling the truth; being unable to own their mistakes and give earnest apologies following wrongful accusations; and intimidating her into saying the pledge of allegiance by slapping her hand, telling her, "Put your

---

[78] All of the incidents, except for three, came from white educators; the other three were of East and South Asian descent.

hand on your heart," and later after the pledge, saying in her ear, "Respect the flag. Respect the country."

As my daughter shared the details of each instance, all of it sounded so ridiculous to me. It's not that I didn't believe her. It's just that it all sounded so archaic. Sounded like we were in the 1940's or something. How disturbing that anyone would let some of these people anywhere near children; and in certain cases, how disturbing that some of these actions were dismissed (or supported) because they came from teachers viewed as kind and well-meaning. On a very basic level, did some of them think creating an atmosphere of fear would make any child want to learn? How many of these teachers mistakenly believed they were teaching our children grit? Teaching patriotism? Do they value critical thinking or are they threatened by it? Did they forget the importance of modelling maturity and professionalism in the classroom? Do they even possess the qualities of patience, empathy, and compassion that would allow them to model such qualities for our children?

Their behavior doesn't only demonstrate a failure to model the characteristics we hope our children will embody. It doesn't only reveal their lack of knowledge about the effective approaches/strategies in classroom management, conflict resolution, critical thinking, student engagement, and behavior redirection. Their actions also make me wonder what type of unconscious biases these educators have toward my child and other Black children (girls and boys) to cause them to behave in such a fashion. What would cause many of them to assume the worst about my child? Our children?

Jawanza Kunjufu's *Countering the Conspiracy to Destroy Black Boys* was one of the first things to pop into my mind. Later, I thought of the research focusing on the disproportionate number of Black boys in the K-12 system receiving harsher disciplinary action (i.e. suspension, expulsion etc.) compared to white boys, not to mention others studies regarding how Black boys are viewed as less child-like in comparison to white boys.[79] I could also recall the research of J.Luke Wood and Frank Harris examining how Black boys are assumed to be academically inferior.[80] However, nothing immediately came to mind about Black girls until I came across a study conducted by Georgetown Law Center on Poverty and Inequality about teachers perceiving Black girls as less innocent and less child-like in comparison to white girls of the same age. The study found, for example, that Black girls were seen as "behaving and seeming older" than their actual age and that this perception of Black girls was in place as early as the age of five.[81] The study suggested a correlation between these perceptions and harsher treatment in schools and law enforcement.[82]

Though it was clear to my husband and I that the source of our daughter's troubles at school was teacher/administrator bias stemming from lack of education/training and a lack of empathy, seeing the Georgetown study connected her experience to a national pandemic of racial bias against Black girls.

---

[79] German Lopez, "Black Kids are Way More Likely to be Punished in School Than White Kids, Study Finds," *Vox,* April 5, 2018, https://www.vox.com/identities/2018/4/5/17199810/school-discipline-race-racism-gao; Philip Goff et.al., "The Essence of Innocence: Consequences of Dehumanizing Black Children," *Journal of Personality and Social Psychology* 106, no. 4 (2014): 526-545, https://www.apa.org/pubs/journals/releases/psp-a0035663.pdf.
[80] J. Luke Wood and Frank Harris III, *Teaching Boys and Young Men of Color: A Guidebook* (San Diego: Lawndale Hill Publishing, 2016), 13. Note: In the *Black Minds Matter* series, J. Luke Wood references the Early Childhood Longitudinal Study on boys in kindergarten where the findings reveal that Black boys, compared to White, Latino, Asian, and Multiethnic boys, had the highest percentage of teachers who labeled them as incapable of learning. See *Black Minds Matter* Replay, Week 7, "Campus Climates," J. Luke Wood, published 10/4/18, YouTube, https://www.youtube.com/watch?v=fz4ZxF0gnrA; "Early Childhood Longitudinal Study Program," *National Center for Education Statistics,* https://nces.ed.gov/ecls/kindergarten2011.asp.
[81] Adrienne Green, "How Black Girls Aren't Presumed to be Innocent," *The Atlantic,* June 29, 2017, https://www.theatlantic.com/politics/archive/2017/06/black-girls-innocence-georgetown/532050/
[82] Ibid.

I wanted Baby Girl to have a positive relationship with school. Instead, she dreaded going to school. I didn't want this for her, especially not as early as her elementary education. Through their actions and inactions, microaggressions and macroaggressions, they demonstrated they were untrustworthy. Each time they falsely accused her of something, got angry, dismissive, or flippant when she asked legitimate questions, didn't believe her, or didn't do anything about an incident, she learned to be cautious when bringing her truths to white people in positions of authority. The irony is that these very people wondered why they weren't trusted. Have administrators at the school and district level (or coordinators of afterschool and summer programs) ever stopped to look into the connection between the unconscious bias and unexamined white privilege of its teachers and the microaggressions experienced by students of color?

My husband and I never taught her that white people couldn't be trusted. And yet how fascinating to see white people teaching her this lesson for us...and so early in life. Their mouths betray them, revealing an ignorance they try so hard to contain. I could almost feel embarrassed for them if their words and actions didn't hurt so much.

Kids are smart. They are observant. They see what's going on around them. As much as white supremacy, patriarchy, xenophobia, Islamophobia, homophobia, and transphobia have reared their ugly heads in the last few years, especially under the Trump administration, it is irresponsible for institutions not to create spaces where their teachers can reflect upon and explore these issues. Given that our children are already affected by this socio-political climate, our educators need to equip them with the tools to think critically and engage in fruitful dialogue about the world around them.

For teachers to serve our children effectively, they need to not only be competent in their subject areas but also need to take honest looks at their positionality, their subjectivity, the very lens(es) through which they live and operate in the world. They need to figure out how these lenses are shaped by their race, ethnicity, culture, class, gender, sexuality, ability, and religion/spirituality and can affect their delivery of the subjects they teach as well as affect their ability to understand the underlying reasons behind the conflicts and alliances between particular groups of students. Educators and administrators need to reflect upon the following questions:

> What ideas or beliefs or omissions about African Americans, Latinx Americans, Asian Pacific Islander Americans, Native Americans were passed down to them by their mothers, fathers, aunts, uncles, grandmothers, and grandfathers? Have they taken time to reflect on these and: 1) decide how these may be congruent or incongruent with their own ideas or beliefs, and 2) choose their own ideas, beliefs, attitudes, and behavior? How would they respond to these questions with regards to the LGBTQ community? The Muslim community? Other marginalized communities?

> As white people, have they taken the time to examine their white privilege (and how white fragility finds support in this privilege) so it doesn't interfere with their ability to give quality instruction to students of all backgrounds?[83]

> As white people, have they studied the history of the construction of whiteness in the United States?[84] Do they understand how white people have been collectively socialized to view themselves as raceless and not see or speak about race in general or race specifically within the context of social justice?[85] Do they realize that not

---

[83] Robin DiAngelo, "White Fragility," *International Journal of Critical Pedagogy* 3, no. 3 (2011): 58, http://libjournal.uncg.edu/ijcp/article/view/249/116. See also Peggy McIntosh, "White Privilege: Unpacking the Invisible Knapsack," *Wellesley Centers for Women, Seeking Educational Equity and Diversity*, accessed July 11, 2018, https://www.nationalseedproject.org/images/documents/Knapsack_plus_Notes-Peggy_McIntosh.pdf.

[84] Pem Davidson Buck, *Worked to the Bone: Race, Class, Power, and Privilege in Kentucky* (New York: Monthly Review Press, 2001), 23-33, 51-64.

[85] DiAngelo, 62-63. See also Richard Dyer, *White* (New York: Routledge, 1997), 1-3.

reflecting on this history and not actively interrupting the cycle of blind silence makes them complicit in white supremacy?

➢ As white women, have they reflected on both their white privilege and their internalized sexism and how the combination may cause them to misunderstand, misjudge, and/or feel threatened by Black girls, thus inflicting the same pain of dismissal and invisibility and rigid gender constructions that they may have experienced in their own childhood or adulthood?

➢ As white men, have they examined their white and male privilege and challenged patriarchal and white supremacist norms so they can serve as a model for their white, male students?

➢ As men, have they challenged rigid gender constructions so they can avoid perpetuating misconceptions about girls and boys?

➢ As people of color, have they bought into the colorblind mentality? Have they reflected on their own internalized racism and how they can potentially project their conscious or unconscious self-loathing on folks within their own ethnic group as well as those from other marginalized ethnic groups? What anti-Black or anti-immigrant sentiments do they quietly harbor…ones that escape when they least expect? Where did this come from?

➢ If they're straight and cisgender, have they examined their own homophobia and transphobia in order to prevent them from alienating the LGBTQ students in their classes? Do they understand that silence about LGBTQ experiences is not equivalent to acceptance or neutrality? Do they integrate these experiences into the curriculum? Have they taught straight, cisgender students how to be effective allies to LGBTQ students?

➢ Have they sought out the training that would allow them to identify students with learning disabilities and/or provide those students with the accommodations they need? Do they know how to speak to students and their families in a way that isn't alienating but is humanizing? Have they taught students without disabilities how to be effective allies to students with disabilities?

➤ Given the rampant Islamophobia in this country, have they made the effort to learn about Islam? Have they welcomed Muslim students and their families to the school? Have they taught students how to be effective allies to Muslim students?

➤ Do they only talk about how ethnically diverse their school is or do they value their students' ethnic identities enough to ensure that their narratives are integrated throughout the curriculum—from language arts and history to math and science? Do they understand that being colorblind and being "nice" is never enough to produce the deep racial and ethnic interconnectedness they might hope for?

➤ Do they know how to resolve conflicts between, for example, Black, Latinx, and Asian Pacific Islander students that doesn't exacerbate historical or current interethnic divides? Do they know how to heal divisions within each community when it comes to gender and sexuality?

It is vital that all those who work with K-12 students of color—whether it be in public (including public charter) or private schools, online or homeschooling programs, afterschool programs, extracurricular activities, or summer camps—engage in self-reflection about their own unconscious biases that can manifest as microaggressions against children and adolescents from marginalized groups.[86] When it comes to just racism alone, who can deny the correlation between a person's unchecked unconscious biases and all the racial microaggressions eventually leading to a child of color's racial

---

[86] Such reflection is also crucial for those working with children and teenagers within the fields of healthcare, mental health, and juvenile justice.

battle fatigue?[87] How much more when we also consider the array of microaggressions rooted in unconscious biases related to gender, sexuality, class, ability, and religion? If the biases and microaggressions of educators go unchecked, countless students will be harmed by their negligence. Secondly, when instructors are not up-to-date with the current research and practices in positive, descriptive acknowledgment (PDA), Positive Behavior Interventions and Supports (PBIS), Critical Race Achievement Ideology (CRAI), Ethnic Studies and Culturally Relevant/Responsive pedagogies, trauma-informed instruction, Culturally Responsive Education and neuroscience, Whole Brain Teaching (WBT), LGBTQ-Inclusive curriculum, Gender-Complex education, deficit versus equity-minded models in education, conflict resolution (especially the difference between transformative and restorative justice), STEAM across the curriculum, mindfulness, and classroom management, their ignorance robs our children of the opportunities to excel.[88]

Attaining these skills won't happen by attending one workshop. It has to be continuous work—work of the mind, heart, and spirit. For public schools, there should be mandatory district-wide, district-organized professional development sessions dedicated to the topics above at least twice a year. Charter schools, private schools, homeschooling programs, afterschool programs and summer camps, should have trainings for their faculty and staff just as frequently.

---

[87] Racial battle fatigue, coined by William A. Smith in 2003, is defined as "the psychophysiological symptoms resulting from living in mundane extreme racist environments." It speaks to the stress experienced by people of color when subjected to constant racial battles in "historically white spaces" and how this "…can become mentally, emotionally, and physically draining and/or lethal from the accumulation of physiological symptoms that oftentimes goes untreated, unnoticed, or misdiagnosed." See William A. Smith, et. al, "Challenging Racial Battle Fatigue on Historically White Campuses: A Critical Examination of Race-related Stress," accessed July 11, 2018, http://rci.rutgers.edu/~wocfac/WOC/resources/challenging_racial_battle_fatigue .pdf. See also Brooke Adams, "Microaggression and Racial Battle Fatigue," *University of Utah*, December 6, 2016, https://attheu.utah.edu/facultystaff/microaggression-and-racial-battle-fatigue/.
[88] Visit www.brokenshackle.net for a list of specific resources.

Becoming a teacher who stays informed about and uses these practices is ongoing work. It is a muscle that needs to develop throughout one's career as a teacher. The hard work and earnest heart required to strengthen this muscle must take place if we as parents are to deem them qualified enough to teach our children.

In addition to training current faculty, attention must also be given to the hiring process and teacher credential programs. As parents, I recommend we call for the following:

➤ The pedagogies mentioned above must be among the minimum and desired qualifications when hiring teachers for faculty positions; we need to raise the standards that applicants must meet in order to effectively serve all students: students of color and white students.

➤ Ensure that the pedagogies above are central to the training of teachers in credential programs nationwide; these programs must include components where both white students and students of color explore their hearts and explore their own unconscious biases that could lead to microaggressions related to race, gender, sexuality, class, ability and religion; for example, this component should allow space for white students to explore experiences of white privilege and white fragility and for students of color, the experiences of internalized racism. Ultimately, the biases born from such experiences can be raised to the level of consciousness so they don't interfere with their teaching or ability to relate to their students.

➤ In order to increase the pool of applicants of color for teaching positions, urge institutions, districts, etc. to engage in greater outreach to candidates from ethnic groups that reflect the diversity of the student population (i.e. ensure that job announcements and/or teacher job fair invitations reach ethnicity-based professional organizations in education). What kind of impact would this have? 1) Students of color, by seeing a teacher who looks like them, will believe that it's possible for them to become a teacher too (if they so desired), and 2) Both students of color and white students will be able to adjust their perception of who they consider an authority figure/educator and gain experience relating to and respecting a teacher who is not white.

*

Being formally educated with advanced degrees, my husband and I are part of a privileged class. We are fortunate that our education, professional experience, and our relationships with other educators have granted us access to language that allows us to recognize, name, and address teacher incompetence or misconduct as well as affirm strong, talented teachers who are doing things right. Often, knowing the language gives you a certain level of respect which can translate into teachers and administrators viewing you as a partner, working *with* you to give your child the best education possible. However, in some cases, instead of getting respect, you're seen as a threat, often dismissed as a crazy parent who "just complains about everything" and is kept at bay. Whether you know the language or not, parents shouldn't have to have advanced degrees before they get respected. You don't need a college degree to be fully aware of when your child isn't getting the education they deserve.

Not every parent has the language, or perhaps the job flexibility to sit down and address issues of teacher training, performance, and accountability whether it be in meetings at the school or the district level. Despite the call for parent involvement, I think in many ways, some institutions implicitly count on parents being too tired or too busy to address these issues…or count on them not knowing the language.

Whatever the case, knowing the language helps because at least you have tools to challenge institutions with. Remember the teaching practices I mentioned above. You can find articles about each topic in the list of resources on my website, www.brokenshackle.net. Learn the language. Understand why these approaches are effective.

These aren't just good ideas that nobody uses. Teachers are using these practices right now; some have been using them for decades without necessarily knowing or using the language above. They are being used in places where teachers aren't afraid to grow and change if it means it will allow them to help their students succeed. They're being used in places where teachers get the support they need from school and district-level administrators. They're also used by teachers who don't get the support they need but do the good work anyway because they see what lights up students' faces and fills their hearts—they pay attention to what draws their students' interest, they prioritize a healthy learning environment, and they value building relationships with their students and their families.

*

I had a fairly decent K-12 education in public schools from the late 1970s to the early 1990s. Overall, I had teachers and guidance counselors who either respected me and believed in my future or at the very least were neutral and did not overtly antagonize me or the class as a whole. I was never left heartbroken by any of my teachers.

But about a month into Baby Girl's 4th grade year, do you know what she told me when I picked her from school one day? Staring at the ground, she said, "Everyday I'm in this school, my spirit dies."

I'll be damned if I sit by and watch a school kill my child's spirit…and most certainly not for an education that wasn't at least as decent as mine. I didn't work this hard to be a first-generation college graduate and later a professor, just to see my own child get an education that's not only barely mediocre but also breaks her heart!

Each year I say to myself, *I hope she gets a good teacher. I hope she gets a good teacher.* I hear many other parents doing the same, and this makes me sick. This means there are so many bad or unremarkable teachers out there that the most one could do is *hope* for a good one. What kind of sense does it make for your child's education to be a gamble?

I won't do that anymore!

.

.

.

That's what I said yesterday and I say it again today, but is my refusal strong enough? Does my will stand a chance against the enormity of colorblind self-righteousness? We can move her out of an unhealthy place and into a healthier one and hope for the best…but is that the most we can do? If so, that just isn't good enough for me.

All that time my husband and I spent emailing and meeting teachers and principals, and all the time I spent attending school meetings, making statements at school board and district meetings, and sharing input with district curriculum directors and school board members, we might as well have used that energy to homeschool our child. You have no idea how badly I want to. Doesn't seem that feasible right now. But maybe in the future. We'll see.

All of this has taught me that a Black child could come from an educated family and could be as brilliant as ever, but if you put that child in a school environment where the institutions and/or district administrators do not create structures that actively combat systemic racism and other systems of oppression and ensure its teachers employ practices that bring about quality instruction and educational equity, then that Black child will fall victim to the negligence of the school and its district, becoming one more statistic to widen the achievement gap…one more that they'll leave behind and forget.

I don't know how much more of this I can take, and I don't know how much more my baby can take. We can't keep fightin' like this every year for the next eight years.

Just keep us in your prayers.

Wishing you well,

Janet

LETTER #12: QUESTIONS

July 26, 2018

Dear Black Parents Visiting Earth:

Growing up, I was fortunate enough to hear enough teachers say, "If you have any questions, please ask. Questions are good because you never know: there could be someone else in the room who has the exact same question as you."

As a mom and educator, I often tell my child and my students the exact same thing; this helps them not be so afraid of asking questions. It also helps them understand that questions are a sign of strength, not weakness. Often students are self-conscious and are taught to believe that questions make them look stupid, when it's really quite the opposite. Questions demonstrate a student's curiosity and desire to understand. They turn things we don't know into things we do know. They are seeds of critical thought. Questions blossom into investigative skills and problem-solving skills; sometimes, they lead to solutions right away or in other cases, they expose more problems and more questions which can eventually lead to solutions addressing the root cause of a problem. Questions are how great discoveries are made and how great movements begin.

Unfortunately, my daughter has not received this message throughout her education. She has learned quite the opposite. Somehow the idea that questions are a good thing got lost over the decades. It seems the ones who ask questions end up being an easy target for anger and impatience. Those who remain silent and ask nothing will never know this type of emotional beating since they're often praised for being quiet and obedient. The ones who do ask—those who've been taught by their parents and guardians that it's good to ask questions—may have the scars inside to show for it.

As an educator who values questions, I find it disturbing when my child's questions aren't respected.

From one parent to another, please pay attention to how teachers respond to your child's questions. Ask yourself: What philosophies do the teachers have about questions and question-asking? Do they interpret questions as an indication of a child's desire to learn and understand or are they automatically interpreted as a sign of inattentiveness or defiance? Do they have certain ideas about the timing of questions—for example, expectations that they come sooner than later—and if so, have they asked themselves if this reflects a student-centered or a teacher-centered approach? How do these expectations manifest themselves in their responses to students? In what ways are their initial responses to students' questions shaped by their upbringing or their formal education? Did they grow up where children were expected to be seen and not heard? If so, have they realized how much this can discourage children/teens from asking questions? Does a student's question get punished through an impatient sigh or comments/questions like:

> *Weren't you listening?*
> *Why do I have to repeat myself?*
> *Why didn't you ask/tell me sooner?*
> *You should have been paying attention.*
> *You should know this by now.*
> *You still don't know?*

When paying attention to and reflecting upon how teachers treat your child's questions, you may discover something quite revealing about their attitudes toward question-asking.

If you or folks in your family respond to your child's questions in some of the ways listed above, you might need to check yourself and each other. When one uses such responses at home, hearing a teacher respond in the same fashion (when addressing your child's questions) might sound normal and acceptable. As a result, one may not recognize the harm it creates. That shit ain't ok.

All of us should wonder what fuels such responses when it would take far less energy (and perhaps even fewer words) to just answer the question. If this is the first internal voice that surfaces, shut it down! Save the sarcasm. Save the anger. Save the impatience. Ensure that everyone, especially our children's teachers, do the same.

These responses to a child's questions are punitive. They reveal impatience and assume there is something wrong with the child. They instill fear in students, giving them good reason to never ask questions. Such people effectively shame children without even realizing it. This is how children are silenced.

Some examples of respectful ways teachers can respond to our children's questions (before one begins to even answer the question) would be the following:

> *Thank you for that question.*
> *That's a good question.*
> *Yes, I'll address that in one moment. Let's finish this topic, and I'll return to your question.*
> *Thank you for bringing that to my attention.*
> *I don't know. But how about you and I do a little research and talk about what we discover.*

Responding to students' questions in this manner is validating and affirming. And most of all, it allows the teacher to <u>earn</u> their students' trust. If the questions require more individualized attention, the teacher can say, "Let's discuss this one-on-one," and then follow-up. In cases where a student is asking a series of questions in a way that dominates the class discussion, then when they raise their hand to ask another question, the teacher can praise them for doing so, and then say "Let me hear from someone I haven't heard from yet. Let's open up the discussion a bit."

In cases where a teacher seems to be at a loss for what to do/say or has responded to our child's questions with disrespect, then we can offer the suggestions above. We, as parents, can to be the ones to teach the teachers— parents as the teacher-trainers. They may not like parents telling them how to properly and respectfully address our child's questions, but hey…they should've respected our child's questions in the first place. If enough of us are demanding the same respect for our babies, we will see a change.

For our children, questions are vital. Given the history of how our narratives have been withheld and distorted, we cannot just accept what is handed to us. Questions hold power, and our continual liberation depends on it.

Love always,

Janet

LETTER #13: EDUCATION AND YOUR CHILD'S WELL-BEING—25 TIPS

October 12, 2018

Dear Black Parents Visiting Earth:

Based on my first 10 years of being a mama, I want to share some tips about nurturing our child's well-being throughout the process of their formal education. This advice is born from things that worked and things that didn't. This is also born from my experience teaching elementary, middle school, and high school students. Some of these tips involve ways we can nurture our babies and keep them strong and loving. Others offer ways we can prevent our children from becoming a forgotten statistic in the educational system. Take, trash, or tailor these tips to your needs. I strongly believe this list will allow us to maintain clear paths for our children so they can reach their goals and dreams. Here it goes:

1. Be with your child. Be with your child. Be with your child. Make it happen no matter what. Have fun! Laugh together! Build memories! Hug and kiss your child! Carve out time for day trips, overnight trips, or maybe just escape for an hour or two. It doesn't have to be big and expensive for it to be memorable. You just need to be together and fully present.

2. Talk with your child. Show an interest in how their day went. Take the opportunity to encourage them. Show excitement in their accomplishments and celebrate; and teach them how to take joy in hearing about the accomplishments of others. Ask them about what

they learned in school. Ask about their friends, class(es), recess. Did someone say/do something funny today (my personal favorite)? Talk about what's going on in your own life. Share your experiences without diminishing theirs.

A good friend and colleague of mine, Willie Cobb, makes it a priority to ask his children, "How are you feeling?" This shows that their feelings are important to you as a parent. Something I learned after watching the documentary *Mask You Live In* was how Steven and his son Jackson created something called "The Male Box." They wrote notes to each other about their feelings and put them in a box. At the end of the week, they read the notes together and discussed them. This is a good way of communicating your feelings when saying them out loud may feel too difficult or awkward.

By talking with our children, we are showing an interest in who they are and who they are becoming. Essentially, you are taking the opportunity to model and practice openness, honesty, and empathy so they know what it looks and feels like.

Keeping communication lines open with your child is vital if you want them to develop trust in you. Please don't buy into the "No news is good news" belief. Be concerned if they have nothing to say to you. Silence could mean many things, but what I fear most is that silence could mean something is wrong at school or in some other area of their life that the child is too ashamed, embarrassed, or afraid to tell you about. Sometimes, it's because they think you won't believe them. Other times, they might worry about being blamed for what happened, or they think you won't hear them out. Ask clarifying questions if necessary. Take time to listen. Don't be quick-to-anger. Children will share with the people they trust. Value their word. Believe them. Believe *in* them. And you'll see, they'll keep coming back.[89]

---

[89] My daughter is now 10. So far, this practice has worked out very well. I'm hoping I am providing the right foundation for her to view me as someone she can

3. Keep a gratitude jar. Each day, on an index card, ask them to write down two or more good things that happened that day—events or moments they are grateful for. Have them put these in a jar. At the end of the week, let them take out the cards and read them. This is a helpful exercise because it can be very easy to forget the good and only remember the bad, especially given the negativity bias of the brain. The gratitude jar allows them/us to remember the good things that happen throughout the week so we can maintain a positive outlook on life.

4. Bring your children to college campuses from the moment they're born. Continue throughout their elementary, middle, and high school years. Let them envision themselves standing on a university campus, feeling a sense of belonging. Allow them to picture themselves graduating from a university, feeling ready to take on the world! Being on a university campus early in life can help make that vision a reality.

5. Enroll your child in enrichment activities aligned with their interests. If there is a set of essential skills you want them to have, expose them early and explain why. At the same time, pay close attention to and support what they enjoy; let their interests guide you as they mature. Be careful not to overload their schedules. You don't want them to think that living a regimented lifestyle and feeling burnt out is a healthy norm. Make sure there's lots of time to play and chill.

6. Get them in the habit of using day planners. I started using the Planner Pad during college. In retrospect, I wish I started using it in middle or high school. I loved their "funnel system" so much that I've been using their planners ever since. After using the system for about 20 years, I decided to have Baby Girl use the same type of planner beginning in the 4th grade. It helps her keep track of important dates, tasks, fun events, and responsibilities. I don't

---

trust throughout her tween and teen years. We'll see. Check with me in about 5-8 years. I may have to tweak this advice a bit depending on how those years go.

recommend being too strict with planners at first because you don't want the planner to introduce headache and heartache. Using a planner is intended to reduce stress, not become a new source of stress. As with everything, be patient with the baby steps.

7. Give your child the tools to advocate for themselves. At the same time, understand that there are many situations where you will need to intervene and defend your child on their behalf.[90] Advocate for your child and they will value themselves enough to advocate for themselves.

8. Show and tell your child that you love them. Hug and kiss them daily. Show and tell them that you are proud of them. Explain how you are proud of who they are, what they do, and how they do it…and share why.

9. When it comes to grades, I have a few thoughts. Though I want my daughter to get good grades in school, I worry about how she's learning to equate her self-worth with her grades. When she tells me she received an 84% on a test and asks me, "Mama what grade is that? Is that good?" The subtext I sometimes hear in that question is, "Am I good? Am I smart? Will you still love me if it's bad?" Throughout my 21 years of teaching, I've watched students draw the conclusion that bad grades mean you are stupid or mean you are a bad person. I don't want that for my child. When it comes to grades, here are some values I communicate to her:

   a. First, I let her know that I will love her through all the A's and F's, the accomplishments and failures, and everything in between. At the same time, I want her to always live up to her potential, rise to a challenge, and be proud of her accomplishments. The latter became particularly important during a period when she wouldn't say too much about how

---

[90] This probably goes without saying especially considering how fast that parental instinct to protect our babies kicks in.

well she did on an assignment because she didn't want to sound arrogant or make others feel bad. My husband's brilliant response to this was, "Never let anyone dim your shine."

b. When she gets A's and B's, I praise her and ask her how she feels about it. I then ask her, "Do you feel like you understood the material?" and "Can you picture yourself teaching a classmate how to do these problems?" or "Can you picture yourself explaining this topic to a classmate?" For me, knowledge is more than just about possessing it or getting a good grade. It's also about realizing the responsibility attached to having the knowledge—that Baby Girl is in a position to share the knowledge so someone else can benefit from and be empowered by it in the same way she has.

c. Regarding C, Ds, and Fs, I've told her that, of course, we will still love her, but will be concerned and will ask her (and help her figure out) what she can do to improve her grade. Secondly, if, for example, we hear that our child received a C on a quiz, and anger and frustration are the first emotions we feel, then we need to take a step back and first ask how many questions were on the quiz in the first place. One of the things I've always hated is seeing student comprehension assessed through a 10-question quiz or test (where each question is worth one point). This leaves little to no room for error. A child gets three questions wrong and their grade is down to a C. Always keep the grade in perspective and help your child do the same.

d. Take comprehension beyond grades. We try to create fun interactive activities (or mnemonic devices) to help her enjoy and remember what she learns. Learning needs to be fun so it will stick. Have your child write stories of imaginary worlds or create songs about something in history. Apply math skills through cooking, baking, sewing, drawing, or making music. Do science projects in the backyard or the kitchen using simple supplies or ordinary objects around the house. If you're looking for ideas, search for free projects online. For an introduction to electronics and circuit building, try Snap Circuits, the Arduino Starter Kit, and visit www.adafruit.com. For culturally situated design tools (rooted in the field of ethnomathematics), visit https://csdt.rpi.edu/culture/index.html. For additional STEAM projects, check out the Exploratorium's online store (www.exploratoriumstore.com), Yellow Scope— Science Kits for Girls (yellow-scope.com) or subscription services like Tinker Crate (www.kiwico.com) and Mel Science (www.melscience.com).

10. By the age of 3, get your child in the habit of reading by using Bob Books or other books appropriate for new readers. By the age of 5, have your child read 20 min/day, write 20 min/day, and do math (from a Spectrum or Kumon workbook) 20 min/day.[91] Starting out, one can always begin with 5 or 10 min/day on each and then slowly work their way up to 20 min/day; this can help to not overwhelm the child; observe your child and let their progress guide you. These times can increase to 30 min/day as they grow older…especially during the summer. (Note: you can also consider having the child write every other day instead of everyday if necessary.) When reading or watching TV or movies, integrate lessons in media literacy whenever you can. Make sure they have plenty of time to play, draw, make things, and explore the outdoors. Chill on the weekends.

---

[91] Though common core standards push nonfiction, please make sure your child reads fiction and poetry; and don't forget to include comic books and graphic novels.

11. Create an inviting, organized study space for your child as early as three but no later than five years old. Here's what you need: desk, lamp, pencil case with pencils and eraser, crayons/markers/colored pencils (whatever is age-appropriate), paper, construction paper, glue sticks, scissors, and a pencil sharpener. As the child grows older, make sure they have filler paper, 3-ring binders, composition books, spiral notebooks, dividers, index cards (on a ring), a 3-hole puncher, and a stapler. Plants, flowers, or scented candles (unlit would be smart) will also help the study space feel inviting. On the walls and on shelves nearby, surround the space with pictures of your child and the family as well as images representing a broad spectrum of accomplished Black folks from different professions.

12. Enroll your child in Kumon's math program (or a comparable math enrichment program) early.[92] Understand that math is a language. If you want a child to communicate in this language, it requires fluency like any other language. Its applications are countless, especially in science and the arts; without fluency, seeing these connections becomes very difficult.

    As a former math teacher, I was incredibly dissatisfied with the poor quality and overall lack of enthusiasm when it came to the math instruction my daughter was getting in public school. After consulting with a couple of friends, my husband and I decided to enroll her in Kumon and overall were very impressed with their 60-year old system.

---

[92] Feel free to enroll your child in the reading program as well. Since our child had more difficulty with math than reading, we decided to keep the cost down by just enrolling her in Kumon math. We are fortunate enough to be in a place in our lives where we can afford the monthly fee; I know as a child, my parents couldn't afford something like this. So, what if you can't afford the fee? What are the alternatives? What can we do to make sure our children get these skills? A couple of recommendations: 1) for families who can't afford the monthly cost, we can create a fund making it possible for them to enroll in Kumon (or a comparable program), or 2) groups of families can organize regular meetings to teach our children these skills for free, creating a space for our children to gain the math or reading skills they need.

When we realized that by the end of the 3rd grade, Baby Girl's math proficiency was below grade level, we enrolled her in the program at the start of her 4th grade year. The math skill and confidence she once possessed in kindergarten and 1st grade quickly dwindled by the end of the 2nd grade and then even more so during the 3rd grade. Within a year at Kumon, she was back up to grade level.

Through doing problems everyday, she regained confidence in her math skills and became more independent. The repetition helped her to develop fluency—something that needs to be developed in math in the same way students are expected to develop fluency in reading. Baby Girl learned the importance of mastering the basics of addition, subtraction, multiplication, and division (along with improving her speed) before moving on to fractions, algebra, and geometry. If these skills aren't mastered, more advanced mathematics will not make sense.

This was an uphill climb for Baby Girl. Lots of tears and frustration that later became smiles and pride. As anticipated, her math skills improved. But what we didn't expect was that she would also learn what it feels like to make progress…that with persistence, she can overcome any challenge.

13. If your child shares an incident with you that took place between: 1) your child and a teacher or 2) your child and another student, please ask your child to write it down right away, making sure to include the date on which the incident took place. This will become helpful when you need to discuss this with teachers, parents, administrators, and/or attorneys. Such details also help when filing formal grievances.

14. Be aware that it is possible for teachers who have been disrespectful, inappropriate, and/or abusive toward students to not be held accountable by the institution. In some cases, it could be because the administrator doesn't sufficiently understand the impact on the child

or because the administrator is not strong or effective enough to correct the teacher's behavior. Sometimes it's because no one knew since the child never told their parents (i.e. for many of the reasons mentioned in #2). Sometimes, children tell their parents, but the parents are too afraid to speak up because they don't want the teacher to retaliate against their child or because they don't want to be labeled as "an angry black (wo)man." Sometimes, the child will tell an adult (i.e. parent, teacher, administrator, office staff) and they are dismissed because what the child has shared is inconsistent with what they believe the teacher is capable of (i.e. especially in the case of a teacher who is award-winning or has a reputation for being nice, approachable, and/or everyone's favorite). In any of these cases, here are a couple options: 1) research ways you can gain access to an educational attorney, and 2) keep your eyes and ears peeled for other parents who might have similar experiences to yours; there is strength in numbers. If multiple parents are filing complaints about the same individual, it's a whole lot more difficult for an institution to ignore the issue, especially if it looks like the situation can turn into a class action lawsuit.

15. Our daughter has been very open with my husband and I. We have demonstrated our love and honesty toward her and she shows us the same. She trusts us, feels safe with us. We are not perfect, but she knows we will believe her and will take action if she brings an incident to our attention.

    Please understand that if you want your child to trust you or any authority figure, then you or that authority figure needs to be trustworthy. A child doesn't have to automatically hand their trust over to any adult. Grown-ups must earn a child's trust. When an incident happens to a child, one can identify a trustworthy adult based on: 1) knowing the person will believe them and 2) knowing the person will do something to make things right (or at least better).[93]

16. When you are trying to get a teacher, administrator, or staff member to take responsibility for their actions, it is possible for the teacher, administrator, or staff to engage in some form of victim-blaming toward you or your child, whether it's gaslighting, recommending your child get counseling, criticizing the way you brought the incident to their attention (i.e. timing or tone), telling your child (after the child has set clear verbal boundaries) that they're just making a situation worse, questioning why the child didn't tell someone at school sooner, or stating the child is harboring a victim mentality or claiming you as the parent have instilled a victim mentality in your child. In such cases understand the following:

  a. A child who has experienced trauma will be very cautious about who they can trust. They know better than to go to someone who may not believe them and risk reliving experiences of confusion, self-doubt, and pain all over again.

  b. We need to take neuroscience into consideration, especially when it comes to children of color experiencing racial microaggressions. Zaretta Hammond, author of *Culturally Responsive Teaching and the Brain*, explains that when one examines culturally responsive brain rules, the primary principle to keep in mind is that, "The brain seeks to minimize social threats and maximize opportunities to

---

[93] Sometimes a child may deem you trustworthy because they feel like you can keep a secret. They may tell you the "secret" precisely because they think you won't do anything about it (i.e. won't tell anyone)—essentially keeping the secret safe. In cases of abuse, sexual harassment/assault, bullying, or self-harm, it is important to understand that what they have shared with you must be reported to the appropriate authorities (i.e. administration, district, child protective services, and/or law enforcement, etc.). When you do report this, be prepared for the possibility that the child may view you as untrustworthy as a result.

connect with others in community."[94] Hammond points out that:

> The brain's two prime directives are to stay safe and be happy. The brain takes its social needs very seriously and is fierce in protecting an individual's sense of well-being, self-determination, and self-worth along with its connection to community. We cannot downplay students' need to feel safe and valued in the classroom, the brain will not seek to connect with others if it perceives them to be threatening to its social or psychological well-being based on what they say and do. It's important to point out that what a teacher may regard as an innocent gesture may be interpreted by the student as threatening. As a result, the amygdala stays on alert, trying to detect other microaggressions.[95]

Someone who poses a threat—ranging from a perpetrator of verbal or physical assault to one who engages in victim-blaming—doesn't make a child (or adult for that matter) feel safe. Such behavior gives them no reason in the future to want to connect with or trust someone who is a threat. Hammond points out that when considering the stress of students from marginalized communities, due to past experience, their "safety-threat detection" antennae is cued up to detect social and psychological threats. She asserts that, "It becomes imperative to understand how to build positive social relationships that signal to the brain a sense

---

[94] Zaretta Hammond, *Culturally Responsive Teaching and the Brain: Promoting Authentic Engagement and Rigor Among Culturally and Linguistically Diverse Students* (Thousand Oaks: Corwin Press, 2015), 47.
[95] Ibid.

of physical, psychological, and social safety so that learning is possible."[96]

    c.   In cases where your child has been victimized by an authority figure (i.e. faculty, staff, administrator, police officer, storeowner, etc.) and your child is labeled as harboring a victim mentality or you are labeled as a parent instilling a victim mentality in your child, tell the person to read Tim Wise's essay, "Racism and the Myth of the 'Victim Mentality,'" and call it a day![97] Understand that when you are trying to get a person at fault to take responsibility for their actions, this is the opposite of wallowing in the despair, feeling powerless, and doing nothing. You are taking action to prevent something like this from happening in the future to your child or someone else's child. You are trying to end the victimhood, not perpetuate it.

17. When bringing issues up to a teacher or administrator like equity, microaggressions, Ethnic Studies and culturally responsive pedagogy, unconscious bias, racial battle fatigue, white privilege and white fragility, gender construction, gender identity and expression, sexuality, toxic masculinity, sexual harassment, disability, religion, and other topics, don't be surprised if there is resistance. Often parents and children are told that school isn't the appropriate place to discuss these issues, that it is unnecessary, or that there isn't enough time/resources since school is meant to focus on "core" subjects like math, reading, writing, science, and history. Don't let that stop you. If the person is uncomfortable/unfamiliar with, and/or perceive the topic as too "controversial" to touch, the person might feel attacked or threatened by you and perhaps even view you as a parent who enjoys stirring up trouble. Understand that a

---

[96] Ibid, 45.
[97] Tim Wise, "Racism and the Myth of a Victim Mentality," *Tim Wise: Antiracist Essayist, Author, and Educator*, February 27, 2010, http://www.timwise.org/2010/02/racism-and-the-myth-of-a-victim-mentality/.

teacher's or administrator's resistance to these issues is a clear sign that an entire shift in consciousness (on the part of the school and the district) is required in order to create a climate that is not only open to and prepared to discuss these issues with its faculty, staff, students, and families, but also open and prepared to incorporate such topics into classroom instruction.

It's possible that as you engage in individual or collective efforts to shift consciousness, you may end up being disliked by parents, teachers, and administrators alike. If it comes to this, you need to be okay with being disliked. Your first priority is the well-being of your child. Secondly, understand that awareness of these issues and how they influence instruction benefits Black students in particular, but also students from all racial and ethnic backgrounds.

18. Watch the documentaries *Miss Representation* and *Mask You Live In* to understand the impact of rigid constructions of femininity and masculinity on our children. Select age-appropriate clips to watch/discuss with them.

19. For starters, read *Why Are All the Black Kids Sitting Together in the Cafeteria* by Beverly Tatum, *The Dreamkeepers: Successful Teachers of African American Children* by Gloria Ladson-Billings, *The State of the African American Male* and *African American Females* by Eboni Zamani-Gallaher and Vernon Polite, *Black on Both Sides: A Racial History of Trans Identity* by C. Riley Snorton, and watch the *Black Minds Matter* course series by J. Luke Wood. Form small discussion groups to talk about how the intelligence, creativity, and emotional well-being of our children can be nurtured.

20. In addition to the resources in #18 and #19, refer parents/faculty/staff/administrators/ afterschool program educators to the full list of educational resources on my website www.brokenshackle.net. You may run into some folks who will be very grateful for these resources and eager to learn from them. Often

these are the ones who are ready to put the new info into practice; perhaps they'll want to have future discussions with you about what they've learned and how they can implement new policies at their institution. You may run into some who are defensive and say they don't have the time or that their teachers aren't perfect "so don't expect us to change anytime soon." Take a mental note and congratulate yourself: you just figured out who your true allies are. Work with whatcha got.

21. You will run into some teachers who are very good at what they do. Strong command of their subject. Charismatic. Animated. Well-liked. Passionate. But when it comes to topics related to social justice (as mentioned in #17 above and in Letter #11 on Education), they believe these things are unnecessary or might overburden teachers and students. If teachers believe that they've had success with their students without addressing these issues, they often assume their teaching is "above" racism and other systems of oppression and therefore transcends injustice. Essentially, such teachers overestimate their own competence when it comes to these issues— typical Dunning-Kruger effect. This makes it extremely difficult to point out how crucial these issues are. These teachers, white and people of color, may very well be kind, extraordinary people, but the blindness to their own bias and shortcomings are hard to break through. They have reached the limits of their skill set and need ongoing professional development in these areas.

22. It is important for us to get teachers to understand that:

    a. Our humanity and the way we experience our humanity emerge from a cultural context; if a teacher with a colorblind mentality says, "Why bring up culture? I treat all students like human beings," then this instructor doesn't actually see the entirety of what shapes a child's human experience and misses an opportunity to engage the class in meaningful ways relevant to the students' lives; in addition to being aware of one's racial biases, teachers must integrate the narratives, experiences, and contributions that reflect the experiences of Black students and other students of color.

b. Niceness is not enough. One must be aware of one's own biases so they don't get in the way of one's ability to be kind. Reflecting on these biases is also necessary order to reach a deep level of kindness that doesn't assume familiarity and doesn't feel intrusive, overwhelming, inauthentic, or uncomfortable to the student.

c. Everyone can have some kind of unconscious bias that undermines justice—whether it relates to race, culture, ethnicity, immigration status, gender and sexuality, class, religion, or disability. No matter if it's silent or spoken, these unconscious biases prevent one from seeing/treating others as fully human; teachers who claim they have no biases don't make themselves any more trustworthy in the eyes of a parent.[98] If anything, it tells me that the teacher hasn't done their personal work to raise their unconscious biases to the level of consciousness.

A teacher must become aware of their positionality, their biases, and the impact of those biases so they don't inadvertently harm students and their families. With time, reflection, and hard work (of the mind, heart, and spirit), we can shed our layers of bias. A beautiful first step is honestly asking one's self how a lack of exposure to particular topics can have an influence on what one's teaches or doesn't teach. Teachers need to seek out course material relevant to the experiences of their students and foster ongoing

---

[98] Though everyone may have unconscious biases, those from the dominant group, no matter what system of oppression under consideration, have a particular responsibility to reflect upon their unconscious biases and raise them to the level of consciousness so they do not inadvertently harm those from marginalized groups.

relationships with the communities that make up their student population.

I don't expect teachers to know everything about our communities or even about their own biases. But I do expect them to try, and I expect them to be honest about what they don't know when parents bring a new perspective to their attention. Hearing responses like, "I didn't realize that," or "I never thought about it that way before," or "Thank you for bringing that to my attention," are helpful. When statements like these are followed by actions taken by the teacher to learn more about your point of view, this shows that the teacher is doing more than just placating you. It is more than alright for us parents to expect teachers to demonstrate cultural humility and an openness to the knowledge parents bring in about our own communities.

d. If a teacher is white or identifies as (or passes as) white, it is crucial for them to understand the history of how white people in the United States have been socialized to not see and critique injustices relating to race, ethnicity, and whiteness—including the ways in which white supremacy have been intertwined with patriarchy, heteronormativity, and class. It is crucial for white people to understand this history and the ways white privilege and white fragility manifest themselves today.

e. Telling us things like, "I put the students' needs first and the parents' second," is divisive, insulting, and alienating. It implicitly pits child against parent, elevates the status of the teacher (with an assumption of "teacher knows best"), and subtly pathologizes us. Such statements reveal a bias that presumes parents are unaware of their own child's intellectual or emotional needs, do not have their child's best interests in mind, and will therefore behave out of selfish interests. It is important for teachers to understand that for Black families (and many other families of color), the child is an extension of the family and the family, an extension of the child. Teachers need to see the child and family as one unit. It is important for teachers to treat parents as partners in the learning process—partners they can learn from and share information with.

23. Always know you have options. Surround yourself with friends to remind you of these options. Don't get stuck in the idea that things are the same everywhere. Just because you're looking for something better doesn't mean you are looking for perfection. Don't get misled by someone who believes that you are. As I mentioned before, we were never searching for perfection. Instead, we were searching for a healthy, responsible, nurturing, inclusive environment. That's the bare minimum our children deserve.

24. Remember that the Supreme Court case *West Virginia State Board of Education v. Barnette* (1943) ruled that it is unconstitutional for students in public schools to be compelled to salute the flag or recite the pledge of allegiance.[99] Secondly, in *Tinker v. Des Moines Independent Community School District* (1969), the Supreme Court ruled that students have the constitutional right to engage in protest during the school day that is not disruptive.[100] Memorize these two cases. Make them roll off your tongue. Keep this in mind in the event that a teacher, administrator, or staff member attempts to force your child to put their hand over their heart and recite the pledge.

---

[99] "West Virginia State Board of Education v. Barnette," *Oyez*, accessed December 22, 2018, https://www.oyez.org/cases/1940-1955/319us624.

[100] "Tinker v. Des Moines Independent Community School District," Oyez, accessed December 22, 2018, https://www.oyez.org/cases/1968/21. See also "NCAC Statement Supports Right of Students to Protest During National Anthem," *National Coalition Against Censorship*, October 10, 2017, https://ncac.org/news/press-release/ncac-statement-supports-right-of-students-to-protest-during-national-anthem.

25. Continue to fight for Ethnic Studies courses in your child's school. Our children need to see reflections of themselves in the curriculum. If you're in California, don't be discouraged by Governor Jerry Brown not signing Assembly Bill 2772—a California bill that would have required high school students to complete an Ethnic Studies course in order to graduate. Remember that Assembly Bill 2016—a California bill requiring the development of an Ethnic Studies model curriculum—passed in 2016 and the development of this model curriculum is currently in progress. In the meantime, band together, make statements at school board meetings (letting them know you are aware of AB 2016), create your own programs, run for school board, email, call, and meet with superintendents, directors of curriculum, and school board members urging them to recognize the benefits of offering Ethnic Studies at the K-12 level. If you're child attends a private school, please do the same. In the 21st century, our children shouldn't have to wait until they're in their twenties before they learn that they come from a long legacy of innovative, brilliant Black folk.

What else can you do now? Don't wait. Be your child's first history teacher and make sure that their knowledge of Black folk extends far beyond slavery, Martin Luther King, Jr., and Rosa Parks. Teach them about: African civilizations; African American townships; African Americans and the Gold Rush; African American political organizations, coalitions, and movements; African American resistance to enslavement; and African American inventors, politicians, actors, directors, filmmakers, scientists, athletes, activists, entrepreneurs, healers, and visual, performing, and literary artists. Teach them about the experiences and contributions of Native Americans, Mexican Americans, Filipina/o/x Americans, Arab Americans, and other communities of color. Centralize our narratives!

Sincerely,

Janet

Letter #14: seeing reflections of the self

July 25, 2018

Dear Black Parents Visiting Earth,

I hope you are well. As I write these letters to you, I remembered a couple things I made for Baby Girl when she was small, and I'd like to share them with you. Because I wanted her to always see reflections of her Blackness no matter what, I did what I could to make that happen. She's 10 years old now and as I look back on these moments, finding and creating spaces where she sees reflections of herself is still necessary, perhaps now more than ever.

*

By the time she turned one, I made a playhouse for her out of a huge cardboard box. It had windows, a door, and even a little awning. I pasted images from Black magazines all over the playhouse. There were famous faces and not so famous faces. She could see Black people doing everything, loving life and being free. I watched her explore the playhouse, looking at the pictures, touching them, slobbering on them, eating them. Forest Whitaker. Danger Mouse. Rosa Parks. Coretta Scott King. Toni Morrison. Ava DuVernay. Michael K. Williams. The Obamas. Gabrielle Union. Kerry Washington.

This playhouse was designed to be her safety net. She had Black people in her life. Of course, she had my husband and I, our friends, and her teachers at daycare who were mostly Black women. But beyond that, we knew that she would encounter plenty of situations where she'd be the only Black child in the room. So, if she didn't see reflections of herself, then at the very least she would have a multitude of dark-skinned and light-skinned faces with nappy, wavy, straight, braided, locked hair imprinted into her subconscious. Her mind would connect:

BLACK

with

historiansactorsentrepreneursdirectorsmusiciansscientistspropertyowners artistseducatorspoliticiansscholarathletesactivistslawyersdoctors

embracinglaughingleadingrunningreadingorganizingdancingwriting speakingjokingteachinglisteningpresentingsmilingposingstudying paintingvotingcampaigninglovinghealing

That playhouse is long gone,
but pieces of it hang on the wall around her desk.
She looks up and knows who she can be and who she's connected to.

*

As Baby Girl's 2nd birthday approached, I wanted her to have little party favors to share with her classmates at daycare. Baby Girl loved Kirikou especially after watching *Kirikou and the Sorceress* at least 10 times. Influenced by West African folklore, this animated film features a clever boy named Kirikou who is able to speak from the moment he's born. He engages in incredibly feats, ultimately saving his village from an evil sorceress named Karaba. Baby Girl watches Kirikou and knows they have a lot in common. They're both busy. Both brave and smart. Both Black. And they both stay winnin'! Since she loved him so much, I decided to create Kirikou book markers and give them to the kids as party favors. It was as simple as printing out an image of Kirikou (with the words "Kirikou is tiny, but he's mighty"), laminating it, punching two holes in the top, pulling faux suede lace through each hole, and creating a knot in each end. The children and the parents loved the bookmarkers and wanted to know more about who this Kirikou was.

I hope you do something like this for your babies. If you already have, I would love to hear about your creations. Talk to you soon.

Your Sister in Spirit,

Janet

LETTER #15: RAISING A MIXED CHILD

July 30, 2018

To Black Parents Visiting Earth,

I was sitting in the grass with a baby in my lap. I was five and that baby was heavy. I was trying to hold his head up and keep from falling over at the same time. The sun was in my eyes. A can of Pringles nearby. Mama and Auntie Lucrecia laughed and laughed as they took pictures of Lance and I. Da'y and Uncle John were playing checkers. We were at Apollo Park that day. This was my earliest memory with the Adderly family.

In the 1970s, there were five Filipino women who found each other in the deserts of Lancaster, CA. They became close friends. All of them Visayan. Two were married to African American men: my mom and Auntie Lucrecia.

Aside from both their husbands being Black, they had many other things in common. They were both from Cebu. Their first names were Lucrecia. And they both had Blackapina(o) children.

Mama and I were always at Auntie Lucrecia's house. While she and Auntie spent time together, Lance and I played everything from airplane and Star Wars to cops and robbers. We played like this for at least seven years until Mama died, and I moved away.

I don't know if Mama brought me there to prevent me from feeling like the only Blackapina(o) kid on the planet, or if my friendship with Lance was just the added bonus that sprang from the good times and good talks she had with Auntie. Could be a bit of both or maybe no conscious decision was ever made. Whatever it was, I am eternally grateful for those years we played together.

As an adult, I can look back and remember that I wasn't the only Blackapina(o) kid around. Though I really wish I met more of us, meeting one other Blackapina(o) child was just enough to fight that feeling of isolation. It reminded me I wasn't some freak of nature…that being mixed—being our kind of mix—could happen more than once.

Twenty-two years later, Auntie Lucrecia found me on Facebook, and Lance and I were reunited. Our families met, and we've been laughing and celebrating ever since…the same way our parents did 40 years ago at Apollo Park.

The impact of those early years are clear now. Today as a mother of a multiracial child of African American, Filipina American, Jamaican, and Puerto Rican descent, I make sure my daughter spends time with playmates who are also multiracial of African/African American descent. I think this is a fundamental way to affirm her mixed heritage and prevent her from feeling like she's the only mixed kid around for miles.

While raising her around other multiracial children, there are some messages that I want to make sure I communicate to her…lessons that I have learned from identifying as Blackapina—a biracial woman of African American and Filipina American descent. Here are some of those lessons.

100% Everything
There was a time when I identified as half Black and half Filipino. I thought this was a good way to embrace both sides of my heritage. But identifying in terms of fractions left me feeling like a bunch of scattered pieces. It seemed to reinforce a fragmented self-perception, as if I was not whole or complete and therefore not "authentic." Using fractions inadvertently brought attention to one of my insecurities: being seen as a diluted or counterfeit

version of my Black or Filipino side.[101] In my twenties, I identified as 100% African American and 100% Filipino American to remind myself (and others) that I was fully both, and that my Black and Filipino blood were inseparable in my veins. In 2007, I began to identify as Blackapina, a blended term signifying being mixed, whole, 100% both at all times, and free of any fear that using such a term would corrupt some pure ethnic essence on either side.[102]

When it comes to Baby Girl, I want her to also see herself as whole. My husband (who is Jamaican and Puerto Rican) and I teach her that she is 100% African American, 100% Filipino American, 100% Jamaican, and 100% Puerto Rican. She is all of these *and* everything in between *and* more. Of course, my husband and I will explain to her that she is technically ¼ this and ¼ that so she knows what side of her ancestral roots comes from where. But conceptually, we want her to understand that she doesn't have to stop being one to live out the other—she is all of these at the same time everyday. As long as she moves in and out of each of these cultural contexts, she will be shaped culturally by each of them; her consciousness will be informed by all of them; she will understand each of them like the beat of her own heart. And she has an entire lifetime to do so. It is our responsibility as parents to seek out opportunities for her to learn about the histories of all four and remain socially connected to all four. Identifying as Black-Filipina-Jamaican-Puerto Rican in name only would yield a shallow, brittle connection to her ancestral past. We hope to see her embody all four roots of her ethnic background and live her life, drawing upon the richness of all four.

One of the beautiful things she will learn about being multiracial is that she has the daily opportunity to draw from a wealth of courage and confidence from multiple homelands at the same time; this allows her to benefit from what her ancestors have left behind for her.

---

[101] Janet Stickmon, *Midnight Peaches Two O'clock Patience* (El Cerrito: Broken Shackle Publishing, International, 2011), 92.
[102] Ibid, 94.

For now, most of those lessons have focused on her African American and Filipino American sides. This has been a good reminder that she doesn't have to look far to learn about her history. Her people(s) have history right here in this country. These lessons will continue as she connects with her Jamaican and Puerto Rican sides in the years to come.

The seeds of these connections have been planted by my husband and I through the books we read to her, the conversations we have, the jokes we make, the gatherings we attend, the stories we tell, the music we listen to, and the shows we watch. It has also been reinforced by her teacher Ms. Cristina Alejo (a.k.a. Tita Tina) who gives her weekly Filipino lessons. Tita Tina has made a conscious effort to not only teach Baby Girl how to speak the Filipino language but also teach her the beauty of what it means to reclaim her language as a heritage speaker. Baby Girl also learns what it feels like to be accepted by someone who values the richness of the four cultures that shape her life experience.

I hope that one day we can bring her to Africa (specifically Ghana, Nigeria, and South Africa), the Philippines, Jamaica, and Puerto Rico. And if we can't bring her to all four, then I want her to always have the freedom to visit once she's left the warmth of our home to make a life of her own. Until then, her homeland will be the family, friends, and spirits from all these places including the United States. May she study, rest, play, and build with her homelands, and be at home no matter what space she steps into.

Just Human?

When Baby Girl was around 8 years old, I remember doing her hair right before school and telling her, "You are Black, Filipina, Jamaican, and Puerto Rican."

Then she said, "and human."

In my head, I was like, *Ok, here we go.*

I said, "Ok, yes, the human part, yes, that's a given. You may not realize it, but many adults say similar things and it implies that any mention of ethnicity is not essential…not necessary. And saying something like this makes people think it's more important to just identify as human."

Brushing her hair, I told her that her humanity can't be separated out from her ethnicities. Being Black, Filipina, Jamaican, and Puerto Rican has and will continue to shape how she experiences the world. Our ethnicity and social class, our gender and sexuality, our ability and religion, and more are interwoven with our humanity. These are amongst the many lenses through which we experience the world as human beings.

I said something to that effect anyway. It sounded good to me, but I wasn't entirely convinced that I was clear enough. I don't think I used all the right words. Maybe they were right for my college students, but perhaps not for an 8-year-old. She said "yes" and "ok" and "uh huh." Perhaps she understood about half of what I said. We'll need to revisit this again…and next time maybe with props. The interconnectedness of social identity and one's humanity requires a little more time and care than a rushed conversation right before school.

*

As I look back on her "and human" response, I was shocked by how quickly it slipped off her tongue. It was only two words. So innocent, so definitive. She was so confident, yet had no idea what was packed into those two little words within the context of race and ethnicity. And of course, how could she? Her schooling never taught her otherwise.

Did she really just say that? Where did she get that from?

This is not something we ever said at home. Ever. I'm not sure if she heard it from TV or at school or somewhere else. Reminds me of how Beverly Tatum describes racism as the smog people breath in the air; just because you can't see how thick it is, doesn't mean you're not breathing it in.[103] I think more specifically, she caught of whiff of some of that colorblind racism Eduardo Bonilla-Silva speaks of.[104]

That kind of racism that believes niceness makes the world go 'round. The type that thinks colorblind racism is a step up from its more blatant counterpart. The type that believes that if we just stop talking about race and racial differences and focus on our sameness—our common humanity—then racism will disappear.

When you come to the United States and hear people say things like:

Why can't we all just be human?

There's only one race, the human race.

I don't see color, I just see people.

#AllLivesMatter

Just know that these things scream colorblind racism.

In and of themselves, these statements/questions/hashtags may seem innocuous and almost virtuous to some. But they reveal a mentality divorced from the real consequences of racial construction. In the words of Robin D.G. Kelly, "Race was never just a matter of how you look. It's about how

---

[103] Beverly Tatum, "Defining Racism: 'Can We Talk?' in *Race, Class, and Gender in the United States*, ed. Paula Rothenberg (New York: Worth Publishers, 2010), 125.
[104] Eduardo Bonilla-Silva, "Color-Blind Racism," in *Race, Class, and Gender in the United States*, ed. Paula Rothenberg (New York: Worth Publishers, 2010), 132. See also Adia Harvey Wingfield, "Color-Blindness is Counterproductive," *The Atlantic*, September 13, 2015,
https://www.theatlantic.com/politics/archive/2015/09/color-blindness-is-counterproductive/405037/.

people assign meaning to how you look."[105] It was about how white elites put structures in place that systematically divided us based on a social construction of race, created a racial hierarchy, uplifting and privileging whites as the ideal. So, when some try to wish race away or ignore it, of course it doesn't work because the structures—meant to divide and establish whites as superior and people of color as inferior—still live and breathe in our institutions and their policies. The consequences of race and racism are felt for centuries after their inception.

Ignoring race, racism, and white supremacy doesn't heal racial divisions and inequities; it makes them worse. And what I find so deeply tragic—something I hear in our children's language but also among adults—is this fear and confusion that any talk about race means one is being racist. There is a lack of understanding that the spaces we operate in are racialized spaces. The silence, the blind eye, again, allow racism to fester. Every time I hear someone accused of being racist for bringing up the topic of race, I can't help but shake my head and think, *That's what happens when we don't teach Ethnic Studies in our schools.*

*

I understand how some folks—white people and people of color—want to emphasize the "just human" part because of the long history of how folks of color were never seen as human beings in the first place…and still today are likened to beasts and aliens and criminals and consequently dehumanized. I get that, but the story doesn't end there. Even though far too many folks need to be reminded that Black folks and other people of color are just as human as white people are, the bottom line is that our common humanity is a given and there are a multitude of ways—that can be named, seen, discussed, and felt—to live out that humanity.

---

[105] *Race: The Power of an Illusion*, Episode 2, "The Story We Tell," directed by Tracy Heather Strain (2003; San Francisco: California Newsreel, 2003), DVD.

The ways we are different from one another should be acknowledged, welcomed, and celebrated because they are opportunities to share with and learn from each other. How shallow and fragile would our relationships be if we only spoke to people who were exactly the same as us? Engaging in exchanges across differences can be enlightening but isn't always easy…and that's okay; though it requires work, it is still possible for unity, harmony, and a peaceful coexistence to be achieved. The level of understanding you reach when acknowledging differences is far deeper than when you try to force sameness and blind yourself to those differences. Remember Audre Lorde's words, "Certainly there are very real differences between us of race, age, and sex. But it is not those differences between us that are separating us. It is rather our refusal to recognize those differences, and to examine the distortions which result from our misnaming them and their effects upon human behavior and expectation."[106]

When the colorblind see me, I say know our similarities, sure, but do not imagine an opaque sameness that hides who I truly am, making it easier for you to look at me. The ways we are different need not be a threat. Differences are good; just don't twist those differences, making them something they are not. Listen. Listen. Ask. Listen. Listen. Differences can be opportunities for understanding and growth.

*

Why do I teach my African American-Filipina-Jamaican-Puerto Rican child about colorblind racism and the value of difference? Judging from the questions she raises at home and at school, the child wants a just world. As it relates to racial justice, I want her to be the type of person who doesn't hide behind her mixed-race identity, believing that her four backgrounds have melted into one non-identity and is therefore above and beyond race. I don't want her mistakenly thinking that by virtue of being mixed, she is somehow exempt from the responsibility of critiquing a system that she may

---

[106] Audre Lorde, *Sister Outsider: Essays and Speeches by Audre Lorde* (Berkeley: Crossing Press, 2007), 115.

benefit from as a mixed-race person, especially being light-skinned. She must have a critical eye if she seeks to understand this world and wants to bring about justice.

Blackness: A Priority
Though my husband and I encourage her to identify with all four of her ethnicities, we make it clear that identifying as multiracial while denying her Blackness is unacceptable.

Since before she was even born, teaching her about her Blackness was a priority. It had to be because my husband and I knew that her Blackness would be the first part of herself to come under attack. The first to be questioned and the first to make her an object of curiosity. We knew this would come from white people and people of color. Instilling her with a sense of pride in her Blackness and African ancestry would prevent her from being broken by racism and internalized racism. As prevalent as anti-Blackness and colorism are, she must be equipped with the knowledge to shut down misconceptions about her African/African American ancestry— and do it quickly.

Light-Skinned: Reflections
Being light-skinned, she'll learn what this means to different people.

She will learn how the mainstream will associate dark skin with being dirty, bad, ugly, stupid, and evil while light skin gets associated with beauty, goodness, innocence, intelligence, and trustworthiness.

Given these messages, we will need to teach her implicit and explicit lessons about valuing the beauty of dark skin and to never tease, insult, or look down upon her darker sisters and brothers for having skin darker than hers. And at the same time, we want her to value the skin she's in.

She will learn about her light skin privilege and how quickly folks will believe her lightness explains why she's pretty, smart, and nice. And then she'll meet folks who won't care how light she is; she'll still be Black enough to be despised.

If her experience is anything like mine, she'll bump into white people who will use her as an informant to help them understand the dark-skinned Black people they're too afraid to approach. She'll run into non-Black folks (white and people of color) who will confide in her because her light skin—and what they believe it means—make them feel comfortable.

Some Black folk will take one look at her and question her loyalties before she has a chance to open her mouth. She'll be seen as "not Black enough" or "not all-the-way" Black—a counterfeit Black girl, destined to be confused for life. And then there will be other Black folk who won't care how light she is—she'll always be Black enough to be welcomed with open arms.

What she has learned so far is this:

> *She calls Daddy chocolate and me oatmeal. We call her nut brown.*

> *The baby knows she's lighter than Daddy and darker than Mama.*

> *One of her friends is Black and Lebanese and is lighter than her.*
> *For a brief stint, they became business partners at the age of 9,*
> *selling terrariums under the company name "Black Girls' Business."*
> *Daddy called them "Light Skin and Light Skin, LLC."*

> *She identifies with the Black kids at school and knows she lies along a spectrum of*
> *Blackness she sees in the classroom. Some Black kids accept her. Some don't.*

To keep her inspired, I have her pay close attention to biracial people like Jesse Williams, Colin Kaepernick, Asia Jackson, and Yara Shahidi—light-skinned, biracial people of African American descent—who advocate for racial justice. Their work makes them good role models for people of color in general and multiracial people in particular…especially the young ones. Being stark contrasts to the Stacey Dash's of the world, they demonstrate how being a high profile, mixed race individual—ethnically ambiguous or not—is no license for silence, apathy, ignorance, or ambivalence when it comes to understanding critical race theory and standing up for racial justice. As an exercise, she and I watched Jesse Williams' acceptance speech for the Humanitarian Award at the 2016 BET Awards and Yara Shahidi's acceptance speech for the Young, Gifted, and Black Award at the 2017 Black Girls Rock Awards, and I asked her to write down reflections about the two speeches. She responded to two basic questions: What was the main message? What does this mean to you? Another time, I led a writing workshop on multiracial identity at a local library for her and some of her closest friends. Exercises like these sparked good conversations about multiracial identity, skin complexion, and justice.

Being Mixed: The Fifth Dimension
Baby Girl being African American, Filipina, Jamaican, and Puerto Rican, I have had many talks with her (usually while doing her hair) about embracing all sides of her heritage. I tried my best to expose her to each side. However, I don't remember ever telling her about the fifth dimension: that space that lies between her four ethnicities. I've never tried to break this down for a 10-year-old child before, but when I do, I hope to convey something like this:

> *You are mixed. You exist at the meeting place of these four worlds. I know it won't be easy staying connected to all that you are, and at times it may feel like a full-time job, but it is and will continue to be a part of your reality. Some of it will require work (i.e. reading and studying your histories, attending mixed race conferences as well as conferences focused on each ethnic group) and some of it will be heart-filled play, spending time with the family and friends who share your multiple homelands.*

The intersection, the in-between space, the interstice, the overlap is your fifth dimension. It is the space where you will straddle and hold multiple worlds in tension and in joy. The fifth dimension gives you the wiggle room to challenge narrow claims like:

"You can't say you're Black and also say you're mixed."
"You're not Black enough, not Filipino enough, not Jamaican
enough, and not Puerto Rican enough."
"You have to choose one."
"Mixed babies will save the world and put an end to racism."
"You are a tragic, disappointing
consequence of the mixing of races."
"You are doomed to a lifetime of confusion."
"You should identify as 'just human' and
not with any of your ethnicities."

Though you may be the object of shock, curiosity, envy, and hate
you need not fulfill anyone's expectations or be trapped by anyone's
assumptions about who you are or who you should be.
You are no walking contradiction, but instead, a living intersection.
This intersection is a sacred place. You will discover who and how
you want to be within this unique in-between space.
The meaning of your four paths will come together
when you stand in the fifth dimension.

Until next time. Wishing you well always.

Sincerely,

Janet

LETTER #16: LIBERATORY TEACHING

September 19, 2018

Dear Black Parents Visiting Earth:

Every Sunday morning, Baby Girl wakes up to hear Tita Tina's melodic voice on FaceTime, "Magandang umaga! Kumusta ka?" It's been a year now since she started taking Filipino lessons with Tita Tina. This helps her stay connected to her Filipino heritage and know what it's like to be in the presence of a passionate, highly skilled teacher—one who has a strong command of the subject matter and also knows exactly how to make her students feel valued and embraced.

Cristina Alejo, affectionately known as Tita Tina in the Filipino American community, has been teaching for 20 years in the San Francisco Unified School District and was a cofounder of Galing Bata After School Program. During her undergraduate years, Tita Tina studied at the University of the Philippines Diliman and worked with Dr. Virgilio Enriquez (a.k.a. Doc E) as a student assistant and later as his research assistant. Dr. Enriquez, the author of *From Colonial to Liberation Psychology: The Philippine Experience*, is known as the father of *Sikolohiyang Pilipino* (Filipino Psychology), researching and identifying indigenous Filipino core values of personhood. His inspiration shines through Tita Tina's dynamic, liberatory approach to teaching.

Throughout her career, Tita Tina has shared her passionate teaching style with students in Pre-K, 2nd grade, 4th grade, and special education as well as students in the Sama Sama Summer Camp—a Filipino cultural immersion camp where Baby Girl first met her. I am inspired by Tita Tina's expertise in culturally responsive pedagogy and neuroscience, restorative justice, positive, descriptive acknowledgment (PDA), and Positive Behavior Interventions and Supports (PBIS) and how well she puts all of this into practice. I've seen her integrate Baby Girl's background knowledge and weekly experiences into each lesson and take the opportunity to incorporate holidays like Indigenous People's Day or demonstrations like March for Our Lives. All of this is done to create greater relevance and retention of the language frames.

Tita Tina came along at a crucial time in Baby Girl's life. Her lessons—interwoven with warm greetings, playfulness, and affirmations—reversed the damage done by teachers in her life, especially those who didn't believe her word, accused of her things she didn't do, or didn't appreciate her questions. During the toughest times in her elementary school education, Tita Tina's presence was an intervention. She interrupted Baby Girl's brokenness and helped her value her gifts, especially her critical mind and her multiracial identity. She was very aware of the prevalence of anti-Blackness (including its presence amongst Filipinos) and always helped her feel accepted for all that she was. Tita Tina often reminded her that she comes from a long legacy of African American and Filipino freedom fighters who questioned authority as they demanded their liberation.

Baby Girl's self-esteem returns as Tita Tina teaches her to say:

> ➤ *Ako ay magaling.* (I am awesome/excellent.)
> ➤ *Ako ay magalang.* (I am respectful.)
> ➤ *Ako ay matapang.* (I am courageous.)

New hope and meaning are given to her experiences as she learns Filipino proverbs like:

> ➤ *Sa isang pintong masarhan, ay sampu ang mabubuksan.* (For every door that closes, ten more will open.)

> ➤ *Sa marunong umunawa, sukat ang isang salita.* (To one who listens and understands, one explanation is enough.)

> ➤ *Kung may itinanim, may aanihin.* (If you plant a seed and nurture it, you will reap the harvest in the future.)

At the end of each session, she tells me what was covered, asks how I feel about it, and shares what can be done in preparation for the next session. Exchanges like this make it obvious that she not only values her relationship with our daughter but also her relationship with us as her parents. She understands that the child is an extension of the family, not a threat to or competition for the teacher. The family is just as much a part of the educational process as the child is—a key factor that so many teachers and administrators completely miss. Essentially, Tita Tina is welcoming us in to share the excitement of witnessing how much Baby Girl has learned. And when we are done speaking, I turn to Baby Girl and see that she is growing stronger and more brilliant right before my eyes.

Tita Tina's actions demonstrate that she's doing everything in her power to pass on the wealth of our ancestral past to the next generation. Every Sunday, she brings to life the very words she shared one night while showing Baby Girl around SoMa Pilipinas: "This culture belongs to you and no one can take that away from you."

Look for teachers like Tita Tina. This is what teaching looks like when it's done right.

Lots of hugs,

Janet

LETTER # 17: MY LAST LETTER (FOR NOW)

October 19, 2018

Dear Black Parents Visiting Earth:

Back in 2008, I thought writing my Master's thesis was the hardest thing I'd ever done until I tried getting my baby off the pacifier. She was only on it from about three months old to six or seven months, but judging from her cries, you'd think she came out the womb with it. Weaning her off the boobie was even harder. I tried and failed when she was a year old, but was finally successful when she was two and a half. My husband potty-trained her when I no longer had the energy to try. And when she learned to tie her shoes, I thought it was a miracle because it felt like it took forever. With those milestones behind us, we then moved on to figuring out where she would go for kindergarten.

As if the first five years weren't hard enough, we were hit with the next five and these years really kicked my ass...not because of Baby Girl but because of the world around her.

I'm still standing though and so is my husband. We can stand because we lean on each other. And thank goodness we have a small network of folks we can call family—folks we rely on to hold us up and make us laugh. I wouldn't have it any other way.

And so how did our kid turn out? Not too bad.

Baby Girl still bursts at the seams with happiness, her giggle and song contagious. She climbs without fear and leaps from high places. She's open and honest. Her clapbacks quicker than ever. She seeks solutions for the world's problems. She's been on the honor roll twice since she transferred schools and manages to terrorize my husband and I by making fart noises with her armpits (and the back of her knees—something I deeply regret teaching her). In short, she's a risk-taker, she takes care of business, and she hasn't lost her ability to just be a kid and play.

Make no mistake: this took a lot of work to preserve and maintain. Her work and ours.

Indeed her joy is still there, but she's jaded now. She's more cautious about who she can trust. She has more skills, but they don't come without scars. She's slowly turning into a social justice warrior much sooner than expected, but I am grateful for this fire and compassion. I was hoping that the innocence of pure play would linger for a bit, but perhaps that's a luxury Black children don't have considering the world being what it is.

This side of her developed more out of necessity, more out of an effort to find meaning in the wrongs that entered her life uninvited. We held her through many tears; there were many nights when we also wept, never wanting her to fall victim to the world's ignorance and injustice so early in life.

I intervened every chance I could get before any of this could sink in. I wasn't always the best at it, but perhaps I was better than I thought. I didn't always feel like it, but it didn't matter because her well-being came first. Together, my husband and I tackled many battles; and for the record, I am a diehard fan of how my husband handled some of the toughest battles our child faced. I'm sure we pissed some folks off, but hopefully they will think about their behavior and seek out resources that reflect the broad perspectives, experiences, and contributions of Black people in this country and worldwide.

Throughout these battles, for the most part, I was clear and intentional. But not always. Often these battles tested my courage. There were times when I had flashbacks of old and not so old moments I thought I'd forgotten. The racial battle fatigue of Black parents is real. Luckily, I had people to talk to so I could feel and process everything; this allowed me to then focus on my daughter and what she was experiencing. I pray my actions were half as good as my words each time I told her none of this was her fault.

If I were to extract a meaningful, redeeming lesson from all this, I would say that I am grateful that Baby Girl could see my husband and I advocating for her, reminding her that she's always worth fighting for. This is crucial if we want her to value herself enough—especially in the future as a teenager and an adult—to fight to preserve her own dignity and well-being so she can flourish and blossom.

Thanks to her inner drive, her undying happiness, her resiliency, and her trust in us, we were able to make sure the world could see her for who she truly is.

After all she's put up with, I look at her and stand in awe. My baby is strong, intelligent, and beautiful!

Our babies are strong, intelligent, and beautiful!

Sometimes Black scars look like excellence. We polish the remnants of battle 'til they're the object of envy. On the surface, it appears as though we are untouched by pain. When the world discovers the story behind the brilliance, the envy stops and the respect begins. The planet stands still to look and bow. People around the globe recognize the emotional fortitude it takes to maintain such brilliance and pray for the same in their own lives.

Though the racial battle fatigue of us parents and our children is real, we continue to press on. The armor we've molded for Baby Girl is one we've molded for ourselves. As our armor grows stronger, I pray our hearts remain soft and earnest.

Hopefully, Black parents throughout the United States and around the world will one day write to you and share their experiences. By reading all of our letters, you will get the fullest view of what to expect and how to raise our children to live meaningful lives in the 21st century.

With all the love I can give,

Janet Stickmon

LETTER # 18: DEAR BABY GIRL

October 20, 2018

Dear Black Parents Visiting Earth:

One more thing. About a year ago, I did a presentation about these letters to you, and a woman asked, "Have you shared these with your daughter?" I was stuck. I said no and stumbled a bit. I never did share them with Baby Girl and in the moment, I had no real reason why.

Maybe it was because I felt like she was too young to understand. Perhaps it was because the letters revealed a frustration and heartache that I didn't want her to see. The woman's question bothered me and made me wonder what my daughter would think if she did read my letters.

The answer to this is difficult to predict, but eventually she'll read these letters and let me know what she thinks. I simply pray I'll be ready for her thoughts and questions when she does.

I also wondered what it would be like to write letters to Baby Girl. How different would they sound compared to what I've told you over the past five years?

I finally stopped wondering and started writing. I pictured Baby Girl as an adult, listening to me tell her stories about her childhood. The funny things. The things that broke my heart. The things I wanted her to remember. I hope that when she reads these reflections, she'll get the same feeling I get whenever I look at all the handwritten labels Mama taped to the bottom of the trophies I won as a child: the pieces of lined paper she carefully cut into pieces, documenting the where, what, and when; the Scotch tape she used to laminate each label so it wouldn't fall apart. Mama put enough time and care into each label because she wanted it last. She wanted me to see it years later and remember. That's love. Though I only had her in my life for 15 years, I can still feel this love 30 years after her death. We can communicate our love through the things we leave behind. So, I'll leave behind these stories for Baby Girl.

If I want you to really understand how it's been being a Black parent of a Black child, a Black mama of a Black daughter, a mixed race mama of a mixed race child, then I can't simply tell you about the experience; you would have to witness our relationship. But since there's no way you could actually be here in our home for the past 10 years, then the next best thing is letting you into my inner conversations with Baby Girl—the ones that existed mostly in my head until now. Perhaps you'll see a different side of us as parents and a different side of our daughter as well.

Here are my stories. I hope they feed your spirit as much as they've fed mine. Most of all, I hope these stories make my baby smile.

I wish you my best. Looking forward to meeting you one day.

Love and Blessings,

Janet

When you were just a couple months old, I brought you to Sagrada in Oakland for the first time. It's an interfaith sacred arts store where I didn't have to look too hard to find reflections of myself. I felt at home there. Soon it became your home and your playground.

I remember feeling empty and disconnected during that visit. I was looking for meaning. I was searching to be reconnected with God. I used to pray the rosary and meditate all the time. I used to do the Examen of Consciousness and the *Lectio Divina*. If I had no words, I simply sat at my altar. But when you were born, there wasn't much time for any of that. But let's be honest: I stopped praying and meditating long before you came along…so, please know that you were never the reason I stopped praying; there was just something about that time that deepened my awareness that my connection to the Creator wasn't what I wanted it to be. I longed for those quiet contemplative moments I used to enjoy.

Bouncing you around that store, I showed you books, candles, crosses, crystals…Black and Brown saints, white sage bundles, Celtic knots. You didn't understand what you were looking at. But then again, maybe you did.

I don't remember what I bought that day, but I went up to the counter, and a woman welcomed me over with a warm smile. Our exchange began with friendly small talk, and later I told her a bit about my spirituality and how empty I was feeling. At some point in the conversation, I told her, "I think I need a spiritual practice." Smiling, she pointed at you and gently said, "I think that's your spiritual practice right there."

*

Your bedtime routine was simple when you were a baby. It didn't always work, but it worked most of time and that was good enough me. I swaddled you, tucked you into the Maya wrap, and bounced you around the house. Daddy dimmed the lights and played the same song for you every night— "Green Forests, Lush Meadows, and Soft Rain Falling" from the Pure

Sounds album. We used to have a wooden rocking chair in the livingroom where I rocked you back and forth, back and forth until eventually you fell asleep. Sometimes…most of the time…you didn't fall asleep right away. You would just stare at me with your big, round eyes…and then started talking. You talked and talked. You always had a lot to say. I never knew what you were trying to tell me but that never stopped you. Especially at bedtime. Your little face and your little habits found their way into a lullaby I sang to you every night:

Go to sleep
Go to sleep
Go to sleep my baby

Go to sleep
Go to sleep
Go to sleep my baby

You like to talk a lot at night
And it's so funny
My black diamond eyes.

Go to sleep
Go to sleep
Go to sleep my baby

Go to sleep
Go to sleep
Go to sleep my baby

You like to talk a lot at night
And it's so pretty
My black diamond eyes.

*

You were 5 months old when I returned to work. I left you with your first
teacher, Ms. Tonya. She was a Black woman, about your same complexion,
with hazel eyes and long brown hair pulled back in a ponytail. She told me I
could call as many times as I needed to. This was perfect because I was
having a really hard time leaving you at daycare.
That first week, I cried just about everyday.
But it was okay because Ms. Tonya knew what she was doing.
She had a soft heart and a solid backbone.

Ms. Tonya taught you how to safely crawl down
from a mattress and onto the floor.
She noticed how you always knew exactly what you wanted.

Ms. Tonya understood your anger and never called it bad and never made
you change it; she knew you'd need it for later.
I remember your Daddy told me how he picked you up
from daycare one day, and Ms. Tonya said,
"Shawn, you got a thug!"
Your Daddy nodded with pride. Ha!
We were proud of that fire in you.

Well, you stayed in the infant room until you were about a year old. Toward
the end, you always took your naps in the toddler swing. On your last day,
right before you were about to transition to the toddler room, you found
some other kid sitting in that swing. You shook that thing so hard, you
nearly tossed his little ass off the swing. Ms. Tonya said, "We need to get
that child out the swing before something happens." She took the other
child out and put you in. Within minutes, you were knocked out. There you
were, lookin' rough with your mouth wide-open, pink and yellow striped
shirt all wrinkled, one pant leg up, and one Adidas shelltoe on.
But you got what you wanted: that final nap in your swing.

*

It never happened when you had to pee. Only when you pooped. There must have been something about sitting on the toilet all alone that made you feel vulnerable and pensive. Like you needed to empty out your heart and soul to someone close by. And that someone was usually me. You would moan and groan and say, "Oh Mama, y' knowwww what happened todayyyyy…" still moaning and groaning. Then all the stories and feelings and thoughts from the day came spilling out.

Toilet confessions. They began when you were around four or five.
I thought they were the funniest thing until you begged me to stay in the bathroom with you. You used to smell like apple pie when you were a baby.
Sweets, you don't smell like apple pie anymore.
Remember how I couldn't always stay in the bathroom with you?
Instead, I sat outside near the door to listen to the rest of your story.
If it was comfort or reassurance you needed,
I hope I was able to offer that from the other side of the bathroom door.
Those toilet confessions were the cutest but so damn filthy.

*

We've been singing songs to you your whole life.
Most of them we made up on the fly.
Crying babies have a way of turning parents into lyrical geniuses.

In the tub, I would sing:

Scrub, scrub, scrub the baby
Scrub, scrub, scrub the baby
Scrub, scrub, scrub the baby
Scrub 'til she's all clean.

In the livingroom, Daddy would sing
(to the tune of "Mary Had a Little Lamb"):

Imani had a big black cat

Dope black cat
Fresh black cat
Imani had a big black cat
Whose fur was black as coal.

In the kitchen, I would sing
(to a tune inspired by "Okra" by Olu Dara):

Strawberries, strawberries
I want some strawberries, strawberries
Strawberries, strawberries
I want some strawberries.
Oooooo!

Blueberries, blueberries
I want some blueberries, blueberries
Blueberries, blueberries
I want some blueberries.
Oooooo!

It's no wonder the music in your heart evolved into songs like
"Booger Man"—a seven-minute Disney-esque-honky-tonk-jazzy song you
freestyled on the toilet. You told the tale of a man, his boogers, his dad
from L.A., his mom from N.Y., and some police officer. Brilliant!

*

The three of us were walking around San Francisco one afternoon. You
were busy eating a hot dog as your Daddy and I took turns pushing you in
the stroller. At some point down Market St., you fell asleep. We went into
Clarks to take a look at shoes. Daddy rolled you around for a bit and
checked out some other stores next door.
This gave me a chance to shop.

The store clerk was no ordinary salesman. He wasn't overtly friendly, but still very welcoming. His name was Jack, and he wore a leather apron. He was a serious man with no fancy airs about him. Judging by the apron and the level of detail he used when he spoke about shoes, he must have been a shoemaker. His appreciation for shoes was much deeper than mine. Jack understood and believed in the craft. He took great pride in the way shoes were made and explained why certain shoes brought greater comfort and support than others. Each time I tried on a pair, he leaned in to see if I liked them, looking at me as if I was tasting a cake he just baked. If I didn't care for them, he was ready with another pair for me to try on. Jack didn't smile much, but he was attentive and kind.
He seemed rare, belonging to a dying breed of storekeepers who valued relationships over profit.

Daddy came back into the store with you. You were still asleep. I was still trying on shoes. Jack came back, holding another pair of shoes and greeted Daddy. Jack looked at you and cracked a smile. You began to squirm a bit, a sign that you were about to wake up soon. Your eyes were still closed, but you started chewing. Your Daddy and I looked at you. We were confused and disgusted. "What are you chewing?" we both asked. You were too drowsy to answer. I slipped my finger into your mouth to see. You were chewing what was left of that hot dog you had earlier. Your Daddy and I just shook our heads and laughed, "That's nasty!"
Judging by the look on his face,
Jack thought so too, but didn't saying anything;
he smiled and walked away quietly, finding something else to do.

I'm not one to care too much about what strangers think, but I was slightly embarrassed in front of this austere artisan. Not like a *my-kid-just-peed-all-over-your-floor* kind of feeling, but more like a
my-kid-just-farted-and-I-hope-no-one-heard-that kind of feeling.
Truly, it was funnier than it was embarrassing.
I'm sure Jack will remember our faces the next time we come back.
But, I'm not sure I wanna be remembered as that family
with the kid who had leftover food in her mouth

good enough for a post-nap snack.

*

Some kids don't wash their hands. Some don't use soap. But you use soap and water, and you wash your little hands really well...but you never dry them. What is that?!! You come out the bathroom with your hands dripping wet like nothing's wrong. I don't get it.

*

You and your Daddy were at Trader Joe's one day. You were about 3 years old. Both of you were standing in line and an old white lady bumped into you and knocked you down. Your Daddy said, "You're not going to apologize to her? You better say sorry to her." The lady said, "I'm not apologizing to a kid." You got up, looked at her, and said, "Ooo, your butt stinks." Your Daddy fell out...and so did the sales clerk and everybody in that line.

*

Baby Girl, do you remember when you were 5 and you got one of those do-it-yourself bracelet kits for Christmas? Did I ever tell you what I did to that box before I wrapped it up? Well, the packaging for these kits always had images of white hands and smiling white girls on them. I was pissed that I could never find one box with a Black hand or face on it. I wanted you to unwrap a gift you really wanted and see beautiful Blackness on the packaging. So, I cut out pictures from *Ebony* magazine and pasted them all over every white face and hand on that box.
Done and done.

*

It was so frustrating shopping in stores that sold girls' pants with fake pockets and fake drawstrings. By the time you were 9, it really pissed you off.

You understood the message manufacturers were sending:
"All that matters is the appearance of pockets and drawstrings.
Girls don't really use these things."
Often, we went to the boys' section to get you pants
with real pockets and drawstrings.

*

Every time I turned around, you made some new contraption.
One time, I woke up from a nap and you were rolling across the floor,
yelling, "Look Mama!!!" You were sitting in a box glued to a raggedy
skateboard. You attached an old belt to the sides to keep you strapped in.

When you were 7—shortly before Ahmed Mohamed was arrested in Irving,
Texas for showing his teacher a clock he made—you found a small circuit
board and attached a bulb, some wires, and a watch head to it, using
electrical tape. The bulb didn't light up, but it didn't matter to you. What
was clear was your desire to build electronics and the belief that you could
do it. You were proud. And so were we.
We knew we had to nurture this love of yours somehow.

By the time you were 5, to add to your bucket of Legos, we bought you
Magformers and later Snap Circuits. That year we signed you up for Mad
Science classes; I think this was also around the time your Ninang Lisa
bought you a microscope. At 7, we got you a science kit to create an
electrochemical clock. Then, at 8, it was Lego Robotics. At 9, you did
Tinker Crate projects. That summer, you learned Scratch and how to use
Blender for 3-D printing. That fall, you went to the Black Girls Code Game
Jam and gained some skills in JavaScript.
And then, you had a couple private lessons in chemistry.

We may not be able to afford these STEAM camps that cost $350-
800+/week, but don't worry Baby Girl, we'll get you the skills you need.
We know your coding, 3-D printing skills, and your interest in circuits
won't get reinforced in school, so your Daddy and I will have to stay on top
of this at home. I would hate for your passion for the sciences to die just

because the school doesn't have a strong enough STEAM program or
because your teachers couldn't see your gifts, or because someone gave you
the idea that girls don't do this type of thing.
Your cousin Chris just recommended the Arduino Starter Kit for you;
that needs to be the next step.
We'll see how it goes.

*

One night, I was reading you a book about
George Washington Carver and learned that
Booker T. Washington died in 1915.
D'ay was 3 or 4 years old at the time.
I knew my dad was old, but goddamn!

*

The first time I went to a conference on mixed race, I was in my early 20s. I
hope that one day you will attend something like this much sooner in life. It
was nice to not feel alone, comforting to be surrounded by folks just as
ethnically ambiguous as me. It was also weird, almost like staring in a
mirror. I felt like one of the Time Haters travelling back to slavery times,
and I was Buc Nasty, locking eyes with one of my ancestors.

*

When you were 7 years old, I made something for you and blessed it with
mystery and spark. It began with a black hardbound sketchbook. I wrapped
it in layers of bark paper, the colors of rust and earth. Mulberry leaves and
dark red roses peeked from the corners and center—cute stickers making
you look twice to see if they were real. The edges reinforced with electrical
tape, allowing the book to withstand perhaps a fall or some other mishap
caused by a sudden release of power from its pages.
When it was complete, I named the book
The Tome of Wonder and Creation.

The tome was created to hold your most brilliant thoughts and visions, as well as all your failures and imperfections. It is where you can experiment, solve problems, and make new discoveries. It is the place for your deepest reflections and wildest stories…with plenty of room for the mundane. Let *The Tome of Wonder and Creation* remind you that anything that begins in your imagination has the power to come to life. Let it remind you who you are and where you come from. I pray you will keep this for the rest of your life.
But just in case it somehow gets lost,
I hope you remember the note
on the first page that was meant just for you:

The Tome of Wonder and Creation

~this sacred text responds only to the touch, voice, and will of its owner~

In this book, you will find Adinkra symbols, Baybayin, and a Periodic Table of the Elements. Study the contents of these pages well. Study them with love and fascination. Please call upon our Creator and all your African, African American, Jamaican, Filipina(o), and Puerto Rican ancestors for their guidance; call them with honor and reverence. Let your curiosity and imagination also be your holy guides. May you fill the blank pages with additional knowledge and wisdom left behind by all those who have come before you, as well as all your descendants who may call out to you. May these pages be the canvas on which you practice writing the symbols and characters and begin using them as the building blocks for new creations of your own. The magical power of the Tome of Wonder and Creation lies in your hard work and your natural gifts and talents. My sweet baby girl, you have all my Love and you have all Daddy's Love. May our Love keep you warm, happy, and inspired to make beautiful, wonderful creations for all living things throughout the universe.

Love Always,

Mama and Daddy
December 25, 2017

*

We underestimated the work involved in bringing a life into the world…the
kind of strain it would put on each of us and our marriage. You weren't the
cause of the strain; never believe that you were; as Dad puts it,
"Childrearing just amplifies the things that may have been lacking in the
relationship prior to the birth of the child." Your Daddy and I learned a lot
about ourselves and how to be better at taking care of each other. There
were many painful, confusing lessons learned. Many beautiful lessons
learned. Lots of cakes eaten, flowers exchanged, and chicken barbequed.
And we are still learning and loving.
You know Sweets, you helped us with that.

Remember when you were small, you brought me over to the top of the
steps near the livingroom and draped your Lola's blanket over my head like
a veil. Your Daddy was sitting on the couch. He and I looked at each other,
wondering what you were up to. You left the room, ran back in, and
handed me a bouquet of plastic flowers;
you told me to walk toward Daddy. So, I did.

Sweets, you were wise enough to understand that we needed this. In that
moment, you reminded us of our vows. You helped us to become better
people and to explore where love could take us.
We are a stronger family because of you.

*

A white art teacher about 70+ years old tells you to sit down like a human
being. When you try to apply a Jackson Pollack approach to your work, you
were told, "That's what monkeys do." As soon as I picked you up, you told
me this, and we turned right back around to confront her about her
language. It was a brief discussion. She couldn't even remember what she
said to you, but apologized to both of us. She said, "I guess I was just
saying what my mother used to say to me."

A young black man in his 20's gives us a tour of Stanford. He listens to you
talk about your interest in the sciences. He listens to me talk about how

worried I was that you might forget the coding, 3-D printing, circuit-
building you learned in the summer since these won't be reinforced in
school. With excitement he says,
"This is perfect! Let's make sure we exchange info.
I want to connect you with a mentor of mine.
He can hook you up."

Both of them drew from what was familiar and
passed it on to you without hesitation.

One made you feel stupid,
spilling into you a poison about a century old.

The other made you feel strong, sharing
his time, his attention, his connections...
seeing himself in you.

*

You were 10 years old and made it to the honor roll for a third time. We
went to Kendajah, a Liberian restaurant in San Leandro, to celebrate.
Daddy asked you, "So how did it feel to get the award today?" The owner
of the restaurant, Dougie Uso, brought some utensils to the table and
overheard the conversation,
"Oh, what award did you get?"
"I was on the honor roll for getting straight A's," you said.
"Oh! Straight A's. Oh," pointing to the oxtail, "your food is on the house!
And what drink do you want? Anything you want! It's free!"
Your face lit up, big smile, as you looked at us for approval.
"The Fanta. The orange soda,"
Dougie came back over with the soda and said, "You know, straight A's,
that's hard to come by. What that means is that you worked very hard.
Keep that up. Keep getting straight A's because when you grow up that
means you can get scholarships, and
your parents won't have to pay for college."

A big smile washed over my face, partly imagining the relief of not having to pay for your college education, but also because Dougie was celebrating your accomplishment right along with us. He rewarded you, praised you. And you were receiving this praise from kin. We came to right place that night.

*

One day, the three of us were walking across the street. You told us that Harriet Tubman died in 1913. Da'y was 1 or 2 years old back then. I knew my dad was old, but goddamn!

*

there is an unspoken understanding between your Daddy and other men, usually Black, but not always 'hood, country, bourgie big and tall, 270+ lbs. and no less with kids in tow or ridin' solo they look each other in the eye and pass by with a nod of respect sometimes silent sometimes *Wassup man?* or *How's it goin' boss?* anywhere: grocery store, post office, movie theatre, farmer's market doesn't matter; always a nod this is Big Man Understandin' an exchange that never happens between your Daddy and small, skinny dudes a little dude wouldn't get it this is a recognition, a common understanding about what it's like to be a big man in this world they don't have to explain; needs no second thought they just know a shared admiration between strangers Big Man Understandin'

*

Saturday, you and I went kayaking in Sausalito with some friends. So much fun! Water splashed on our feet. We saw harbor seals and house boats and a gang of seagulls that took over an abandoned boat.

Your Daddy drove to Santa Rosa for Comic Con. Before he could get there, he was pulled over by the cops three times in 45 minutes. He told me later this was called batoning.

Four days later, I was washing dishes and you were drawing in your bedroom. Your Daddy went to Target to get you pajamas and some toilet paper. Daddy saw two Black kids around 10-13 years old, putting Lunchables under their sweatshirts. Your Daddy told them not to steal the food; he'd buy it for them instead. He handed them some money, and they put the food back. A group of loss prevention officers surrounded them. One grabbed your Daddy by the shirt. Daddy tried to explain, and one told him to shut up. Your Daddy reminded him that he wasn't a real law enforcement officer and said, "I could run over and through you and there'd be little you could do about it." Your Daddy then told him to shut up, explained what happened, and told him he was going to purchase the food for the kids. One said, "These type of kids need a hard lesson." Your Daddy said, "You're right, but that lesson should be compassion and empathy, not hardassness."

*

Dealing with silly instructors and classmates, you endured and confronted more than any child should. Your Daddy and I are so very proud of how hard you've fought. We're proud of the attitude and skills you've developed while defending your dignity: the awareness of your self-worth, the quick wit, quick hands, the way you hold students and teachers accountable. You know you are a treasure, so you defend and protect that treasure. You know we will listen to you, believe you, believe in you, support you. We've shown you what love, affection, kindness, gentleness, good teaching, healthy boundaries, and a

sense of humor look like through our own actions and those actions of the
loved ones we've allowed into your space.
When the antithesis of this crosses your path,
you recognize it and speak on it.

The actions of some of your school teachers amounted to a wasted
opportunity—they missed out on the chance to be moved by you, the chance
to build a healthy relationship with you. They wasted a chance to affirm and
validate you…and be remembered as that teacher who encouraged you and
kept you strong. We left you, our baby, in their trust for over six hours each
day thinking that at the very least they wouldn't harm you.
Instead, they were careless with your heart and mind
and left you broken.

Beauty, you fought well. You clapped back in more ways than I can count.
And for this and many other reasons,
your Daddy and I will always be proud of you.

But, why should any 9-year-old fight this hard to defend her dignity when
you're just trying to learn how to read, write, and do math? Though you are
an emotionally resilient child, I know that constantly defending yourself
eventually chiseled away at your spirit. I watched it wear you down, causing
you to doubt yourself, crying and wondering, "Why does this keep
happening to me?" My stomach tightened every time I picked you up, and
you had a new incident to tell me about; I had to be quick to reassure you
that it wasn't your fault…that you did nothing to bring this upon
yourself…and remind you, *No, you don't deserve this.*
Luckily, I saw you regain your strength.

As I watched your true self return, I see that their efforts to break you
failed. They didn't understand that your first middle name was Assegai, the
Zulu spear I told you about. If they did, they would have learned from your
courage and understood why your words cut them with such precision each
time they tried to break you. They didn't understand that your second middle
name was Lunasan, a Tagalog word meaning "to heal." If they did, they

would have learned from you as you helped your classmates and became that child so many confided in, laughed with, listened to. They didn't know that Maya Angelou's words, "…I go forth along and stand as 10,000," echoed in your ear each morning I whispered them to you before the bell rang.

They had no idea who they were foolin' with. They had no idea.

*

We went to McDonald's in Richmond, and you were frustrated with the Happy Meal toys. "Why are the girl toys always princesses or something and the boy toys are more active and fun?" You already knew the answer since we had many conversations about rigid gender constructions before. I said, "You should just ask." You looked a little hesitant. I whispered, "It's okay, go ahead. This is your chance," Then I said to the guy behind the sales counter, "My daughter has something to ask you." Then you jumped right in and asked the question, clear and confident.
The young man was Latino, maybe late teens, early 20s. He said, "Well, I think this has to do with society's social norms about girls and boys, but really you can get whatever you want."
Good and succinct. Mama was satisfied with this answer. Funny how your questions get more thoughtful responses at McDonald's than at school.

*

After the service, I went up to Rev. Michael Bernard Beckwith to see if we could get a picture with him. He said sure, and looked at you and complimented your MIT sweatshirt,
and said, "Look at these beautiful eyebrows! They're amazing!"
and stroked his thumbs across them.
Later on, you joked around telling me,
"I think he stretched my eyebrows apart by about an inch.
Look! Can you tell?"
Anyways, he asked what you wanted to be.
You said you wanted to be an engineer.
He prayed over you and sealed your intention to be an engineer

and to reach all your dreams.

Within a couple minutes, your ability to become an engineer
was affirmed and validated.
Your thick eyebrows were called beautiful.

If anyone doubts your ability to become an engineer
or anything else you want to be, please remember this moment.
When anyone questions the beauty of your eyebrows
and tells you to pluck them, please remember this moment.
Rev. Beckwith saw the beauty and magic
that your Daddy and I see in you everyday.
I am so happy you had the chance to meet him.

*

The summer before the third grade,
we signed you up for Camp Destiny—
a summer camp at Destiny Arts in Oakland. Remember?
At the end of your first week of camp, there was a showcase. Tons of
parents filled the room. You were nervous and so were we, but you did just
fine. All the kids from the sun and moon group were havin' a ball!
Honestly, I don't remember exactly what moves you did, I just remember it
was cute and my heart was full. You meditated, you danced, you did martial
arts, you shared your artwork, you performed in a skit.
Throughout the showcase, Hip Hop culture shined through.
Social justice shined through.

Bryan Massengale, the Center-based Programs Manager, made an
announcement. It was his first year in charge of the camp, but it didn't
matter because his heart spoke to us as if he'd been there for years. "I just
want to thank all of you for trusting us enough to leave your children here
all week, for seven hours a day." After two years in private school and one
year in public, not one teacher or administrator ever shared anything like
this with us. It meant so much to hear someone acknowledge the level of
trust it takes for parents to leave their children in
someone else's care all day long.

For the next two summers, we signed you up for Camp Destiny again and
later a Saturday Hip Hop dance class. From the moment you walked into
the building, there were people outside the entrance, inside the entrance,
and down the hallway, welcoming us in and leading our child into the right
studio. They don't just welcome the child, they welcome the whole family.
With this "culture of welcome," initiated by the Artistic Director and one of
Destiny Arts' cofounders, Sarah Crowell, we always felt guided.
I never felt like we, as a family or you in particular,
had to fend for ourselves in a space that was new to us.
And even when we weren't so new, we always felt seen.

Then, we saw you blossom. Sweets, you became more and more confident
with each year. I'll never forget the day you told me, "Destiny Arts is the
only place where I never have problems." That's because Destiny Arts
understands what it means to accept Black children for all that they are,
embracing the mosaic of shades, shapes, sizes, personalities, hair textures,
genders, and sexualities that make up our community. They taught you
about Capoeira, #blacklivesmatter, preferred gender pronouns, Jean
Michel-Basquiat, and Malcolm X.
I was hoping you'd get that from school, but you didn't. Nonetheless, I'm
happy you got it from somewhere. It does my heart well to know you have
one place where you can be yourself and
see yourself in your surroundings.

*

Our collective trauma across the globe, across time, hits me in surges when
I'm not looking. I could be in the classroom, in my car, at home. Sometimes,
I'm on the receiving end of cinema screens or radio waves. There were three
distinct moments I remember weeping uncontrollably: once after watching
Hotel Rwanda, another, watching *Tears of Sun*, and the last while listening to
radio broadcasts about
the survivors of Hurricane Katrina.

Then there was a fourth time I wept.

This time, not because of horror, but because of joy.

Black Panther awoke within me new possibilities. It was the beauty, the strength, the multidimensionality of Black characters on screen: Shuri as scientist and jokester; Nakia as spy, brave and cunning; Okoye, a general, strategic and fearless; the Dora Milaje, fierce warriors, dark- to light-skinned Black women, bald and stunning, bold and strong; women whose lives did not revolve around a man's interests or approval; T'Challa and Killmonger needing each other to know what was true and what was needed;
T'Challa, a reminder that a king can feel
afraid and unprepared, but
IF he makes room for the guidance and expertise of those around him,
including that of his ancestors,
THEN he will always be ready.

Wakanda was Africa without the disruption of colonialism and enslavement—wealth, technology, tradition existing side-by-side; technological advances need not exist at the expense of tradition. Watching T'Challa buy buildings in Oakland to create the Wakanda International Outreach Center…Whoo! That did it for me! From start to finish, this film was unapologetically African. And rightfully so. Thank you for holding me as I sobbed in yours and Daddy's arms. *Black Panther* was the medicine I needed.

I'm so happy this movie came out in your lifetime. Its possibilities are a part of your consciousness now. You have options today that you did not have even a few months ago. And I can see it take hold when you wear shirts and headbands with images of Black Panther, Shuri, Nakia, and Okoye or when you dress up as one of the Dora Milaje for Halloween.
A new world is slowly building in your heart and mind.
I can't wait to see how it turns out.

*

You feel the world around you. You observe and see. You are sensitive to
injustice, especially the kind that hurts Black and Brown kids (girls in
particular), homeless people, and gay and trans folks. You are disappointed
when people make assumptions about you. You hurt when your friends and
classmates are mistreated. You hurt when grown-ups don't bother hearing
your side of the story. You hurt when people don't believe you. You can tell
when grown-ups make excuses for the wrongdoings of others. You are sad
and angry when adults treat children like garbage…or like a number. You
can see what's missing and what needs to be fixed. Your young mind
searches for ways to make life better for more people.
Your Daddy and I listen to you and wonder where
exactly you will fit into all of this.

You expose what others dismiss. You are vocal. You are honest.
You are respectful. You are a peacemaker.
You console the broken and snap at bullies.
Your Daddy and I see your righteous anger well up within you,
and we are there to help you channel this into action.
A trusted few have also helped. Only those who understand are able
to appreciate this fervor and praise you for it.
Remember the words of Audre Lorde, one of the beloved ancestors:

…to my sisters of Color who like me still tremble their rage under harness, or who
sometimes question the expression of our rage as useless and disruptive (the two
most popular accusations)—I want to speak about anger, my anger, and what I
have learned from my travels through its dominions…Every woman has a well-
stocked arsenal of anger potentially useful against those oppressions, personal and
institutional, which brought that anger into being. Focused with precision it can
become a powerful source of energy serving progress and change. And when I
speak of change, I do not mean a simple switch of positions or a temporary
lessening of tensions, nor the ability to smile or feel good. I am speaking of a basic
and radical alteration in those assumptions
underlining our lives.[107]

---

[107] Audre Lorde, "The Uses of Anger: Women Responding to Racism," in *Sister
Outsider: Essays and Speeches by Audre Lorde*, (Berkeley: Crossing Press, 2007), 127.

Those who don't understand your anger will say it's all in your head and will
do their best to keep you quiet. Sweets, just remember Audre Lorde's words
and stay strong. When you speak mountains and build castles, there will be
winds that will try to throw you off. When you defend yourself or others,
there may be times when you will be accused of having (or reinforcing in
others) a victim mentality; and the irony of it is that often in the same
breath, the person(s) at fault will claim to be the real victim. It happens
between strangers. Friends and enemies. Between coworkers. It could
happen at school or at work. In any field. It's an old tool. Textbook case.
People of color seeking justice have been accused of this for centuries. It
continues to keep white people in denial about the culpability of institutions
and those in power whose actions and inactions
produced the systemic injustice in the first place.
Holding people accountable for the ways they mistreat you or others does
not mean you have a victim mentality. In fact, to get perpetrators to take
ownership of their actions is precisely the opposite of harboring a victim
mentality. You are choosing not to wallow and do nothing; instead, you are
taking action. Accusing a victim of having a victim mentality while ignoring
the systems that allow widespread injustices to fester and create more
victims is one of the most emotionally violent claims to ever leave
blithering mouths.

Sweetheart, I know this warning won't take the sting away.
Just because it comes as no surprise doesn't mean it won't hurt.

An accusation like this creates a foul turbulence in the soul, causing you to
doubt everything you thought was real. Being accused of having a victim
mentality is a nice defense for the guilty—it frees them from the
responsibility of ever having to examine flaws in the structures
they build, inherit, and benefit from.

Don't let this keep you from speaking.
Because speaking, exposing, holding people accountable means you are
seeker of justice…that you desire an end to pain.
And sweetheart, this is a good reason to fight.

But before you leave for battle, wear the armor your Daddy and I made for you. You'll need this to protect your heart when you fight.

I saw your heart break several times.
God, I worried that you'd stay broken.
I gave you pep talks, prayers, surprise gifts of donuts and flowers, hoping some of this would work. Only you can tell me if it did. After all the nights you and I both sobbed and tossed and turned,
I don't worry as much as I used to.

Because I've seen you clap back. You've told people:

"You shouldn't speak to me that way."

"Do you like it when I ask questions?
Because when I do, you always sound mad."

"Why did you assume that we would talk the whole time?"

"Are you taking our friendship for granted?"

These words made me smile. When I turned to you and asked,
"And then? What did they say?"
you didn't always remember what they said.
It was as if their response was irrelevant.
You said what needed to be said and that's all that was important.

You don't allow yourself to hurt in silence. You don't excuse bad behavior. You hold mirrors up to their faces so they can see what you see. It's exhausting, yes, but you do it because you are aware of your own value.

I am a little more at peace now because you know how to fight back.

So, press on Baby Girl! Press on.

*

Beauty, I love your heart. At 10 years old, the compassion you have now is the kind that adults spend decades trying to learn. When you cry, I smother you with hugs and kisses. I hold you when you curl up in my lap like a baby. Nearly everything I've said to you in these moments I've forgotten, but I remember always resting my palm on your heart.
Been doing that since you were a baby. And still do, 10 years later.
I love you.

*

You are an Assegai. Use your warrior spirit wisely. You need not wave your spear all around. Your enemy need not see you coming. You don't need to fight all the time. A warrior strategizes and knows when to fight and when to stand down. No need to bring unnecessary attention to yourself, but also know there is no need to hide.
Let your greatness speak for itself.
Assegai, in hand or not,
claim your space,
stand firm in your truth,
own your power.
Ashe.

Janet Stickmon is a professor of humanities and faculty director of the Cultural Center at Napa Valley College. She is the author of *Crushing Soft Rubies—A Memoir, Midnight Peaches, Two O'Clock Patience—A Collection of Essays, Poems, and Short Stories on Womanhood and the Spirit,* and *Male Strippers as Healers and their Emcee as Griotte—Why Magic Mike XXL is Deeper Than You Think.* Stickmon's essays have appeared in *The Huffington Post, Mutha Magazine, Read to Write Stories, Positively Filipino,* and *Red and Yellow, Black and Brown: Decentering Whiteness in Mixed Race Studies* (Rutgers University Press, 2017). Stickmon is the founder of the Black Leaders and Mentorship Program and an educator trainer with Acosta Educational Partnership. Janet Stickmon holds a Master's of the Arts Degree in Ethnic Studies from San Francisco State University, a Master's of the Arts Degree in Religion and Society from the Graduate Theological Union in Berkeley, and a Bachelor's of Science Degree in Civil Engineering from the University of California, Irvine. For over 20 years, Stickmon's work as an educator, writer, and performer has influenced thousands of adults and teens across the country.

For workshops, speaking engagements, and products, visit:
www.brokenshackle.net
 Broken Shackle Publishing, International
 @Blackapina1

Printed in Great Britain
by Amazon

67748729R00104